A PRIMER OF LIBERTARIAN EDUCATION

JOEL SPRING

A PRIMER OF LIBERTARIAN EDUCATION

Black Rose Books
3934 St. Urbain
Montreal 131, Quebec

A PRIMER OF LIBERTARIAN EDUCATION

First Edition

This edition published in Canada by
  Black Rose Books
  3934 St. Urbain
  Montreal 131, Quebec

Published in the United States by
  Free Life Editions, Inc.
  41 Union Square
  New York, N.Y. 10003

ISBN 0-919618-61-8 Paperback
ISBN 0-919618-62-6 Cloth

Canadian Shared Cataloguing in Publication Data

  Spring, Joel H
    A primer of libertarian education

  1. Educational sociology. 2. Education -
  Aims and objectives. I. Title.

  LC189.S73   370.19'3
  ISBN: 0-919618-62-6; 0-919618-61-8 (pbk.)

A NOTE ON THE ILLUSTRATIONS

The illustration on the cover and those used inside this
book are reproduced from linoleum cuts made by children
of the Modern School at the Stelton Colony, Stelton, New
Jersey (1911-1953).

CONTENTS

Introduction 9
1 The Radical Critique of Schooling 13
2 Ownership of Self 33
3 The Growth of Consciousness: Marx to Freire 61
4 Sexual Liberation and Summerhill: Reich and
    Neill.................................. 81
5 Freeing the Child from Childhood 111
6 Present Realities and Future Prospects 129
Notes.. 147
Bibliography 155

A PRIMER OF LIBERTARIAN EDUCATION

INTRODUCTION

LIBERTARIAN THEORIES of education are a product of the belief that any successful radical change in society partly depends upon changes in the character structure and attitudes of the population: a new society cannot be born unless a new person is born that can function within it. Radical pedagogy is concerned with new forms of socialization that will encourage non-authoritarian and revolutionary character structures. Thus, radical pedagogy encompasses not only traditional modes of learning within the school but also methods of child rearing and the organization of the family.

In considering radical forms of education it should be recognized that they have stood *outside* the dominant streams of educational development, which have been directed at reforming society rather than radically changing it. For instance, public schools attempt to eliminate poverty by educating the children of the poor so that they can function within the existing social structure. Radical education would attempt to change the social attitudes which support this social structure. The questions raised by radical education are very different from those raised by a reform-oriented education. The distinction is very much like the one Wilhelm Reich made between radical and reactionary psychologists: a reactionary psychologist, when confronted with poor people who are thieves, would ask how one could end their stealing habits; a radical psychologist would ask why all poor people do not steal. The first approach would emphasize changing behavior to fit into the existing social structure while the second would try to identify those psychological characteristics of the social structure which keep most poor people under control.

Public schooling and radical education are almost contradictory notions. Public schools are supported by the dominant social structure and in turn work to support that structure. Public schools can reform and improve but they do not attempt to make basic structural changes. The rejection of the public school represents one of the important themes in the historical development of radical forms of education—from William Godwin in the eighteenth century to Ivan Illich in the twentieth—and has been premised on the idea that schools came into being as a means of shaping the moral and social beliefs of the population for the benefit of a dominant elite. Throughout the nineteenth and twentieth centuries, this tradition of criticism has been interwoven with practical attempts by radical groups to create a system of education that would free people from ideological control.

This volume focuses on the major radical educational ideas flowing from anarchism, Marxism, and the Freudian left. Anarchism represents one important radical tradition which has attempted to develop techniques for making people free of all domination. As the anarchist Max Stirner emphasized in the nineteenth century, the primary problem is getting people to the point of truly owning their minds. Another radical tradition has sought to achieve freedom from ideological control by raising levels of consciousness and linking thought and learning to social change. This stream of thought has made the overcoming of human alienation in the modern industrial world the first step in radical change. It has its origins in Marxist thought and is best represented in the modern world by the work of Paulo Freire. A third tradition, that of the Freudian left, including people like A.S. Neill and Wilhelm Reich, has emphasized the necessity of changing character structure. All radical educators in the nineteenth and twentieth centuries, of course, have placed some emphasis on the necessity for changing the family structure and liberating women; for some, like Reich, the elimination of the traditional family and the development of free sexual relations were to be the first step in radical education.

All of these groups and ideas have formed a tradition of radical education in the nineteenth and twentieth centuries. It is a tradition which has not necessarily been held together by common contacts, though this did occur, nor by common institutional connections. Rather, its cohesion derives largely from a common belief that power and domination by social structures depend on child-rearing practices and ideological control, that the power of the state and economy rests on a submissive population. Radicals within this tradition have not only a shared critique but a shared alternative vision as well, emphasizing women's liberation, sexual freedom, new forms of family organization, and the importance of autonomy.

Ida Blechman

1
THE RADICAL CRITIQUE OF SCHOOLING

AN IMPORTANT ELEMENT of radical concern about education has been the reaction to the rise of mass schooling in the nineteenth and twentieth centuries. During this period there was a steady trend toward universal compulsory schooling in state-supported and regulated schools. The purpose of mass schooling has been to train the citizen and worker for the modern industrial state. It is only natural for those who seek a radical transformation of society to have adopted a highly critical posture toward systems of schooling which are organized to maintain that society.

The major themes of radical criticism have centered around the political, social, and economic power of the school. One concern has been that public schooling under the control of a national government inevitably leads to attempts by the educational system to produce citizens who will be blindly obedient to the dictates of that government, citizens who will uphold the authority of government even when it runs counter to personal interest and reason and who will adopt a nationalistic posture of "my country, right or wrong." Another theme of radical criticism has been that systems of schooling have been used to produce workers who are trained by the process of schooling to accept work which is monotonous, boring and without personal satisfaction. These workers accept the authority of the industrial system and do not seek any fundamental changes in that system. Still another concern has been the myth of social mobility through education that has accompanied the development of mass schooling. This myth has led to the acceptance of educational credentials as a just measure of social worth and as a basis for social rewards, and yet these credentials have been distributed according to existing social class divisions. Rather than increasing mobility, education has added more cement to the divisions between social classes.[1]

These themes are illustrated by the work of three major critics of education: William Godwin, Francisco Ferrer, and Ivan Illich. Godwin was one of the first critics of education to argue against the political power the state would derive from its ability to spread its particular ideology in the schools. Francisco Ferrer directed his concern toward mass public schooling and its role in producing well-trained and well-controlled workers for the new industrial economies of the nineteenth century. Ivan Illich represents one of the most recent critics of the relationship between schooling and the social system. All of these themes will take on added meaning in later chapters because in one sense radical theories of education have been attempts to produce the *opposite* of the very things these critics are attacking. Radicals have searched for an educational system and a process of child rearing that will create a non-authoritarian person who will not obediently accept the dicatates of the political and social system and who will demand greater personal control and choice.

DURING THE LATE eighteenth and early nineteenth centuries Western societies were feeling the tension of the shift from monarchical to republican forms of government. During this period the close relationship between the political process and mass public schooling was developed. It was at this time that William Godwin wrote his trenchant critique of mass schooling. The French and American revolutions symbolized the eighteenth-century faith in individual reason and its ability to guide government. But there were certain inherent contradictions in these political changes. Faith in individual reason could lead to an argument for no government at all rather than a republican form of government. For William Godwin, born in 1756, the reduction in the power of monarchies seemed to be followed by the increased power of a *new* ruling elite. To change the form of government meant very little as long as any government existed which could be used in the interests of a controlling group. For Godwin faith in the power of human reason implied a society where each person could be sovereign rather than a republican society with periodic changes in the ruling class.

Godwin was born into a family of non-conformist ministers in England. He was trained for the church, but rejected the ministry and in 1783 attempted to open a school. When his school did not succeed, he tried his hand at writing. In 1793 he published an *Enquiry Concerning Political Justice* which is considered the first modern anarchist attack on the concept of the state. Four years later he published the first modern libertarian text on education, the *Enquirer*. In 1796 he married Mary Wollstonecraft whose book *The Vindication of the Rights of Women* is still a classic treatise on women's liberation and the method by which education is used to enslave women to men.[2]

Godwin's ideas must be understood within the framework of the Enlightenment's faith in progress as a product of the unfolding of human reason. He feared that the two most striking phenomena of his time—the rise of the modern state and the development of national systems of education to produce citizens for that state—would have the effect of dogmatically controlling and stifling human reason. In the pamphlet he issued at the opening of his school in 1783, he argued that the two main objects of human power were government and education. The most powerful of the two was education because "government must always depend upon the opinion of the governed. Let the most oppressed people under heaven once change their mode of thinking, and they are free."[3] Any mode of government gains its legitimacy from the recognition and acceptance of people. Control of public opinion through education means continued support. Despotism and injustice can therefore continue to exist in any society in which the full development of human reason has been denied within the walls of the schoolhouse.

The power of national education was clearly defined in Godwin's study of government, *Enquiry Concerning Political Justice*. He warned that "before we put so powerful a machine under the direction of so ambiguous an agent, it behooves us to consider well what it is that we do. Government will not fail to employ it, to strengthen its hands, and perpetuate its institutions." Godwin believed that the content of national education would be shaped to conform to the dictates of political power. He argued that "the data upon which their conduct as statesmen is vindicated, will be the data upon which their instructions are founded."[4] The concern about national education was a reflection of his own suspicions about the nature of government. First, Godwin felt that political institutions favored the usurpation of power by the rich and tended to aggravate the differences between the rich and the poor. Legislation protected the property of the rich by unfair laws and systems of taxation. Law was administered by the government to the advantage of those with economic power, and government enhanced the power of wealth by translating it into social and political power. Second, Godwin believed that the growth of large centralized states would result in the promotion of values, such as a quest for national glory, patriotism, and international economic and cultural competition, which would be of little benefit to the individual:

> The desire to gain a more extensive territory, to conquer or hold in awe our neighbouring states, to surpass them in arts or arms, is a desire founded in prejudice and error. . . . Security and peace are more to be desired than a name at which nations tremble.[5]

National education would be used to support chauvinistic patriotism and the political and economic power of the state.

Godwin had other objections to national education. He wrote,

> It is not true that our youth ought to be instructed to venerate the constitution, however excellent; they should be led to venerate truth; and the constitution only so far as it corresponds with their uninfluenced deductions of truth.[6]

Godwin was convinced that a just society could only be the result of all people freely exercising their reason. Since people were constantly improving their reasoning powers and their understanding of nature, their understanding of the natural laws of conduct was constantly changing. Constitutions and other political institutions which tended to make laws *permanent* could only hinder the unfolding of people's understanding of how life should be regulated.

It was for this reason that Godwin objected to a national education which taught the laws of the land. Most people, he argued, could understand that certain crimes were injurious to the public. Those laws which stood outside the realm of reason and had to be *taught* rather than understood were usually laws which gave advantages to some particular group in society. Godwin wrote, as an example, "It has been alleged, that 'mere reason may teach me not to strike my neighbour; but will never forbid my sending a sack of wool from England, or printing the French constitution in Spain.' " He maintained that "all crimes, that can be supposed to be the fit objects of judicial administration, are capable of being discerned without the teaching of law." He admitted that "my own understanding would never have told me that the exportation of wool was a crime," but, he added, "neither do I believe it is a crime, now that a law has been made affirming it to be such."[7] In this statement Godwin was expressing his own revolutionary conviction that people should not obey laws which did not conform to individual reason.

Godwin warned,

> Had the scheme of a national education been adopted when despotism was most triumphant, it is not to be believed that it could have for ever stifled the voice of truth. But it would have been the most formidable and profound contrivance for that purpose, that imagination can suggest.

Even in countries where liberty tended to prevail, he argued, people should be wary of national education because of its tendency to perpetuate error. In one of the most striking expressions of the case against modern schooling, Godwin declared: "Destroy us if you please; but do not endeavor, by a national education, to destroy in our understandings the discernment of justice and injustice."[8]

Godwin, however, was unique in raising such strong objections during a time when national education was considered one of the most advanced social causes. Even Mary Wollstonecraft favored a national education as a means of eliminating the social advantages of men over women. Godwin's critique was borne out by the facts: most government plans for education *were* directed at maintaining political and social order by instilling particular conceptions of law and morality; most of them *did* place emphasis on building national spirit and patriotism and were viewed as the bulwark of government. Yet most reformers and revolutionaries of the period supported national education plans because of a belief that schooling would sustain individual freedom.

Throughout Western society the modern national state instituted citizenship training in the school. In Prussia, Johann Fichte argued that the state should expend as much money on education as on national defense because,

> The State which introduced universally the national education proposed by us, from the moment that a new generation of youths had passed through it, would need no special army at all, but would have in them an army such as no age has yet seen.[9]

Fichte believed that the school would not only be an instrument for instilling the law of the land but would prepare individuals to sacrifice themselves for the good of the community.

In the United States the prophets of the common school movement argued that a common school would create a consensus of political and social values and effectively reduce political and social unrest. They exhibited an almost limitless faith that the school, regardless of its political control, would become a great engine for freedom and human progress. For example, Henry Barnard, one of the great American common school reformers of the nineteenth century, expressed awareness of the problems caused by state control of the schools, but dismissed them arguing that in the end education always led to freedom. In poetic terms he expressed the faith of the nineteenth-century schoolman in the power of learning once it is set loose in a society. "It would be easier," he wrote in reference to the government stopping the well-schooled individual, "to return the rain to the clouds, from which it is falling, before it has freshened hill-top and valley, mingled with the waters of every rising spring, and reached the roots of every growing plant."[10]

The faith of the nineteenth-century schoolman was certainly crushed in the twentieth century with the rise of Nazi Germany. Schooling in Germany during this period exemplified all the evils Godwin had foreseen in the eighteenth century. Schools were used to spread a particular ideology and a brand of nationalism linked to territorial expansion and to the glorification of the country's leaders. The Nazis implemented changes in the school curriculum, with compulsory training in racial biology and increased emphasis upon German history and literature. Five hours a day of physical education were required for building character and discipline and as preparation for military training. Highly propagandized textbook material was introduced. An order from the Minister of Education in 1935 gave specific instructions to begin racial instruction at the age of six years, to emphasize the importance of race and heredity for the future of the German people and to awaken in the students a pride in their membership in the German race as the bearer of Nordic values. The instructions stated, "World history is to be portrayed as the history of racially-determined peoples."[11]

While Nazi Germany might represent an extreme example of what Godwin had warned against, his criticisms also proved prophetic in the case of the United States—the system of schooling that Leo Tolstoy referred to as the "least bad." Patriotic exercises in U. S. schools reached a fever pitch during the 1920's under pressure from such groups as the American Legion and the Daughters of the American Revolution. Radical labor unions complained about their inability to get union information into the schools and about the schools' emphasis on an economic philosophy opposed to unionization. Upton Sinclair, after touring the public schools in the 1920's, complained that they were not furthering the welfare of humanity but were designed merely to keep the capitalists in power. One of the directors of a radical education program in New Jersey in 1925 declared that

> the public school system is a powerful instrument for the perpetuation of the present social order with all its injustices and inequality ... and that, quite naturally, whatever is likely to disturb the existing arrangement is regarded unfavorably by those in control of the public schools.

Radicals argued that in each community, elected school boards were controlled by a business and professional elite. Studies throughout the century tended to support this conclusion.[1][2]

Whether in Nazi Germany or in the United States, clearly the school by its very nature had become an institution for political control. Since it was an institution consciously designed to change and shape people, it was continually being sought as a weapon by different political factions. By the twentieth century all political groups wanted to use the school to spread their particular ideology and mold their ideal of the modern individual. The problem for radicals was that they usually lacked the power to compete for control of the schools; hence, the schools tended to become bastions of conservatism.

BY THE END of the nineteenth century it seemed that the schools were also beginning to function as appendages to the new industrial economies. It was charged that the schools produced obedient servants of both the state and the corporation. One of the leading critics to make this argument was the Spanish anarchist and educator Francisco Ferrer, who founded the Modern School in Barcelona in 1901. Ferrer's work gained international recognition in 1909 when he was accused by the Spanish government of leading an insurrection in Barcelona and was executed. His execution elicited a cry against injustice from many groups in Europe and the United States and sparked interest in his career and ideas. In the United States a Ferrer Society was organized and a Modern School established in Stelton, New Jersey as well as in other places. In Europe the International League for the Rational Education of Children, which had been founded by Ferrer, was reorganized after his death with Anatole France as its Honorary President. The International League attempted to continue the publication of Ferrer's review, *L'Ecole Renovée*, and distributed information and manuals on the Modern School. In the United States the Ferrer Society published a journal called *The Modern School* which became a vehicle for radical criticism of the schools.

"They know, better than anyone else," Ferrer wrote in reference to government support of schooling, "that their power is based almost entirely on the school."[13] In the past, governments had controlled the masses by keeping them in a state of ignorance. With the rise of industrialism in the nineteenth century, governments found themselves involved in an international economic competition which required trained industrial workers. Schools triumphed in the nineteenth century not because of a general desire to reform society but because of economic requirements. Ferrer wrote that governments wanted schools "not because they hope for the renovation of society through education, but because they need individuals, workmen, perfected instruments of labor to make their industrial enterprises and the capital employed in them profitable."[14] Ferrer recognized that the hierarchical structure of capitalism required certain types of character traits in workers. They had to be trained to accept the boredom and monotony of factory work and to conform obediently to the organization of the factory. Workers needed to be punctual, obedient, passive, and willing to accept their work and position.

In Ferrer's mind the schools had accomplished exactly the things Godwin had warned of in the previous century. In becoming the focal points for maintaining existing institutions, schools came to depend on a system and method which conditioned the student for obedience and docility. This, of course, was a charge leveled at the schools by a variety of critics; from Ferrer's point of view, however, it was an inevitable result of a school controlled by the state. "Children must be accustomed," Ferrer wrote, "to obey, to believe, to think, according to the social dogmas which govern us. Hence, education cannot be other than such as it is to-day."[15] For Ferrer one of the central problems was to break government's power over education. Reform movements that tried to work within the system could accomplish nothing toward the goal of human emancipation. Those who organized the national schools, Ferrer claimed, "have never wanted the uplift of the individual, but his enslavement; and it is perfectly useless to hope for anything from the school of to-day."[16]

For Ferrer it was inconceivable that a government would create a system of education which would lead to any radical changes in society. It was therefore unrealistic to believe that national schooling would be a means of significantly changing the conditions of the lower classes. Since it was the existing social structure which produced the poor, education could eliminate poverty only by freeing people to change the social structure in a radical direction. Writing in a bulletin of the Modern School about the mixing of rich and poor in the schools of Belgium, Ferrer stressed that "the instruction that is given in [the schools] is based on the supposed eternal necessity for a division of rich and poor, and on the principle that social harmony consists in the fulfilment of the laws."[17] What the poor were taught, according to Ferrer, was to accept the existing social structure and to believe that economic improvement depended on individual effort within the existing structure.

Ferrer's criticisms were directed at the very existence of national systems of schooling. Like Godwin, he saw the inevitable use of the school as a source of political control. Schools were becoming a great battleground in which each faction attempted to use the schools for its own ends. "All sides know the importance of the game," he wrote, "and recoil at no sacrifice to secure a victory. Everyone's cry is 'for and by the School.' "[18] The two dominant groups in this battle were government and industry. The government wanted the schools to produce loyal citizens, and industry wanted obedient and trained workers. From Ferrer's point of view these demands were not in conflict. Like Godwin, he believed that the state existed to protect the interests of the rich and that the needs of industry found expression through the state. The differences between the criticisms of Godwin and Ferrer reflect the social differences between the late eighteenth and late nineteenth centuries. The late eighteenth century witnessed the triumph of the nation state, with its demand for loyal citizens. The late nineteenth century witnessed the triumph of the industrial revolution, with its demand not only for trained workers but also for workers who would perform hours of tedious drudgery on the assembly line of the factory. Within this context the goals of schooling were to be accomplished both through the *content* of the material taught in the school and the *method* of presentation.

THE QUESTION OF METHOD became a central concern for these educators. They held that there was a direct link between methods of teaching and school organization, and the type of character molded by the school. Godwin, for instance, argued that it was the method of discipline and the techniques of teaching that undermined reason and eroded human freedom. He made a direct link between the form of motivation used by the teacher and the power of the government. A teacher used *extrinsic motivation*, presenting material to the student "despotically, by allurements or menaces, by showing that the pursuit of it will be attended with . . . approbation, and that the neglect of it will be regarded with displeasure." Extrinsic motivation was defined as that which is connected to a thing by accident or at the pleasure of some other individual such as grades, or threats of punishment. Government, Godwin believed, *also* depended on extrinsic motives to assure that people acted in a certain manner. Laws and police were the despotic means by which government assured that people would act in the interests of the state. An education based on the despotic methods of extrinsic motives prepared the individual for a government of despotic laws.[19]

In the United States the great debate at the beginning of the twentieth century centered around the type of social and economic characteristics produced within the classroom environment. Liberal educators rejected competition and individual work as promoting laissez-faire individualism. They sought a greater emphasis on group activity and group projects. This method of teaching, it was argued, would mold the type of character required by the new corporate state. Radicals in the United States rejected not only the traditional classroom but also the liberal quest. Both sought to mold the student in accordance with the needs and authority of state and industry. One of the directors of the Modern School in New Jersey wrote in the 1920's,

> From the moment the child enters the public school he is trained to submit to authority, to do the will of others as a matter of course, with the result that habits of mind are formed which in adult life are all to the advantage of the ruling class.[20]

The question of the type of methods used in the classroom includes the degree and nature of authority. The schools of the twentieth century have developed a form of anonymous authority which prepares students for manipulation by a bureaucratic and propagandistic society. The traditional classroom exemplified *overt* authority where the teacher directly confronted the students with his or her power and students were at all times aware of the source of power. The redeeming factor in this situation was that if students wished to rebel and claim their freedom, they could identify the source of power and react to it. In the twentieth century anonymous forms of authority were introduced into the classroom through the use of more sophisticated psychological techniques for control. These forms of control have made the realization of manipulation and identification of the source of control extremely difficult.

The issue of the methods of the modern classroom and its relationship to control and authority is elucidated in the writings of Ivan Illich. Illich accepts the radical argument that the techniques used in the classroom in both the nineteenth and twentieth centuries were related to shaping a character that could be manipulated by the existing institutions of authority. The changes in classroom techniques were directly related to changes within these institutions. Illich argues that a modern consumer-oriented society requires a type of character which is dependent on the advice of experts for every action. Modern society depends on the consumption of expertly planned packages. The school prepares the individual for this society by assuming responsibility for "the whole child." By attempting to teach automobile driving, sex education, dressing, adjustment to personality problems, and a host of related topics, the school also teaches that there is an expert and correct way of doing all of these things and that one should depend on the expertise of others. Students in the school ask for freedom and what they receive is the lesson that freedom is only conferred by authorities and must be used "expertly." This dependency creates a form of alienation which destroys people's ability to act. Activity no longer belongs to the individual but to the expert and the institution.[21]

RADICAL CRITICS HAVE also been concerned about the type of character that is developed within the educational process; this concern goes beyond the classroom and into the whole area of child rearing and the nature of the modern family. For instance, psychoanalyst Wilhelm Reich believed that the basic problem in character formation was the structure of the middle-class family. In discussing the rise of fascism in Germany, he linked the authoritarian personality with the process of child rearing within the middle-class German family. Significant social change, he argued, could only take place by changing the family. This theme was echoed throughout the nineteenth and twentieth centuries and, as we shall see later, was an important ingredient in many radical education plans.[22]

Criticism was also leveled at the school insofar as it tended to reinforce and strengthen the social class structure of a society. This problem was debated in almost all educational circles in the nineteenth and twentieth centuries. In the United States educators continually wrestled with the problem of organizing an educational system that decreased the separation between social classes. American educators in the nineteenth century were always quick to criticize European systems for providing different schools for different social classes. Horace Mann, the great common school reformer of the nineteenth century, hoped to overcome this problem by establishing a common school that would be attended by children of all classes. Mann thought that with the rich and the poor rubbing shoulders in the common schoolhouse, class distinctions would melt away. The problem with the common school approach was that not all children entered the school with the same cultural background and intellectual tools, nor did they intend to use their education for the same purposes. In other words, the common school provided the student with *too common* an education. By the end of the nineteenth century American educators were trying to overcome this problem by "individualizing instruction" and "meeting individual needs."

The attempt by American educators to solve the problem of social class highlights one criticism made by Ivan Illich, namely, that the public school as a central institution of socialization tends to *reinforce* the social organization of the surrounding society. In this particular case the school tends to increase social stratification. The attempt to meet "individual needs" in American education—through ability grouping, vocational tracking, and special programs—raised all the contradictions and problems inherent in the school. Ability and vocational grouping were based on intelligence tests, interest and achievement tests, and counseling, with the result that by the middle of the twentieth century there was great concern that American education was discriminating on the basis of social class and race. During the 1940's sociologists studying a small American town found that there was a direct correlation between social classes and vocational tracks in the high school. Children of the town's upper class dominated the ranks of the college preparatory program and children of the lowest class in town filled the vocational track.[2][3] This pattern appeared throughout the United States. And when children were separated according to ability as defined by standardized tests they ended up being grouped according to social class and race. In America children were schooled into their social places almost as if there were separate schools for each social class.

For Ivan Illich this process of social stratification is inherent in schooling and is one of its most destructive features. During the 1960's, while Chancellor of the Catholic University of Puerto Rico, he realized that despite the amount of money the underdeveloped countries of Latin America were spending on education, the poor were not reaping the full benefits of these expenditures. For people to get a full return on the educational dollar they had to go through the whole process of schooling, from the early grades through the universities.

The poor are led to believe that schools will provide them with the opportunity for social advancement, and that advancement within the process of schooling is the result of personal merit. The poor are willing to support schooling on the basis of this faith. But since the rich will always have more years of schooling than the poor, schooling becomes just a new way of measuring established social distances. Because the poor themselves believe in the rightness of the school standard, the school becomes an even more powerful means of social division. The poor are taught to believe that they are poor because they did not make it through school. The poor are told that they were given the opportunity for advancement, and they believe it. Social position is translated through schooling into achievement and underachievement. Within the school the social and economic disadvantages of the poor are termed underachievement. Without the school there would be no dropouts.

Like Francisco Ferrer, Illich views the school as a prostitute of power. The ultimate power, he believes, is the school's effect on one's self-concept; that is, education teaches individuals about their own personal ability and character traits. People learn to think of themselves as stupid or bright, as being worthy or as being failures. Assuming that an adequate self-concept depends on acceptance and on ability to function in a social context, the psychological power of the school is obvious. The school dropout is told essentially that the school—that most helpful and democratic of institutions—has given him or her all opportunities and she or he has failed. The dropout cannot help but accept this failure and conclude that there is little he or she can now do to get ahead. Rejection by the school leads to submission, apathy, and in the end to complete helplessness and social stagnation.

The authority of one social class over another is also strengthened in this process. The school teaches that those with more schooling are better people. Illich argues that the poor learn in school that they should submit to the leadership of those with more schooling, namely the upper classes.

Ivan Illich describes the school as the new church. Society's support of schooling as a religious faith reflects one of the central concerns of radical critics. The school derives its great power from the fact that it has become the central child-rearing institution in modern industrial societies. Early childhood education and day-care centers are slowly increasing the power of this institution, while the role of other institutions in the process of child rearing, such as the family and church, has slowly been eroded.

IN SUMMARY, the very existence of the school allows for its use by a particular political and economic ideology. The content of what is taught depends on who controls society. But the power of the school extends beyond its propagandistic role. The socialization process of the school shapes a particular type of character which meets the needs of the dominant power within the society. For critics like Godwin and Ferrer, the socialization process of the school molds citizens who will submit to the authority of the state and function as loyal workers in the new industrial society. And the socialization process schools people into an acceptance of their social position and makes them dependent upon an irrationally organized consumer society.

Iditha Gale

2
OWNERSHIP
OF SELF

OWNERSHIP OF SELF is an important concept in radical theories of education because it extends the idea of freedom, taking it beyond its usual meaning of political liberty and equality before the law, and emphasizing control over one's beliefs and actions. Political liberty has little meaning if an individual's actions are guided by an internalized authority from which there is no escape. This internalized authority can be the result of the moral imposition of a religion, an education or a child-rearing process. Certainly one of the goals of most educational systems has been the internalization of beliefs and the development of a conscience that will give unquestioned support to the existing social structure. The search for ownership of self has been directed toward finding an educational method or institutional arrangement that would allow for freedom from internalized authority and ideological domination. This has led to experiments with non-authoritarian methods of education.

The concept of ownership of self emerged from the rationalistic background of the eighteenth-century Enlightenment. The Enlightenment brought a revolt against moralistic preachings and religious dogma which hampered the free use of reason. In the nineteenth century arguments were directed at both the state and the church and included a concern with ideology and the alienation of thought from action. This concern revolved around the Marxist argument that the dominant ideology of a society is the ideology of the dominant elite. Ideology is not a product of the actions of the vast majority of a society, but of the needs and desires of one particular social class. Since ideology gives shape and meaning to knowledge, this results in a separation of thought and action. Knowledge becomes something which uses people rather than being used by them. For example, Francisco Ferrer argued in the late nineteenth century that a knowledge of arithmetic could either become a tool for individual use or a tool of enslavement to the industrial system. If arithmetic were taught in terms of the ideology of capitalism—dealing with such things as problems of interest rates, business computations, and other techniques for functioning within the capitalist system—knowledge became a tool for enslavement. On the other hand, if arithmetic problems involving the development of new economic systems were presented, it became a tool of freedom and action.[1]

Since internalized forms of authority constitute a strong barrier to ownership of self, they have been a major concern of radical critics from Rousseau, to Stirner, to the present day. Traditionally, Christianity referred to internalized authority as "conscience" and viewed it as the presence of God's guidance and law within each person. In the late nineteenth century, church, school, family, and community customs were all viewed as important sources for the internalization of beliefs which help maintain social order.

ONE OF THE EARLIEST educational plans to deal with freeing the individual from the domination of a system of internalized prescribed beliefs was Jean Jacques Rousseau's *Emile*, written in the eighteenth century.[2] This work is certainly not as radical as that of the nineteenth-century anarchists but it did foreshadow many of their ideas and is a valuable aid to understanding the later arguments of men like the German anarchist Max Stirner. Rousseau's educational plan was based on the psychological argument that an individual was incapable of reasoning about moral and social problems until the age of adolescence. Any teaching of moral and social ideas *before* this age resulted in acceptance on the basis of authority rather than reason. Rousseau recommended isolating the child from these problems and building the child's early education around a future use of reason. The problem of isolation became an important issue among libertarian educators in the nineteenth and twentieth centuries. Was it really feasible to isolate the child from any dogmatic teaching? And what do you teach if you are isolating the child from all dogma? As we shall see, this became an important problem for anarchist educators like Francisco Ferrer.

According to Rousseau, the individual during this early period of development was incapable of reasoning about morality or social relations. Words like "duty," "obey," "command," and "obligation" should be banished from the vocabulary during this stage of life. An adult should not confront a child with any claim of authority or duty, but with the simple reality that the adult is stronger and older.

For Rousseau the important thing was to avoid any

35

moralistic situations before the age when the child could handle them with his or her own powers of reasoning. This was an important aspect of what Rousseau called "negative education." In this case it meant no moral instruction. If moral instruction were given at an early age, it would dominate action rather than be utilized by the individual. The second part of negative education was the avoidance of verbal learning. This meant education through experience and not through verbal instruction or reading. Rousseau felt that books were one of the great plagues of childhood. He did not mean that the child should not be taught how to read, but rather that learning to read should be attached to experience and necessity. For example, Emile in Rousseau's book would receive invitations to dinners and parties and couldn't find anyone to read them to him. From these experiences Emile would take it upon himself to learn how to read because of self-interest and necessity. Rousseau's method of teaching reading avoided moral instruction—it wasn't based on a sense of duty or belief in some abstract good. Learning and knowledge were tools for the individual to use, not tools to use the individual. As we shall see in the next chapter, this is a major emphasis in the pedagogical methods of Paulo Freire.

The same idea guided the education of Emile just before the stage of adolescence. Rousseau argued that following the law of necessity came the principle of utility. Embodied in this principle was the sacred question, "What is the good of that?" During this stage Emile was introduced to the usefulness of social relationships while avoiding their moral aspects. By learning about the manual arts and occupations, Emile learned about the interdependence of society and the usefulness of social organization. Emile learned about the importance of social organization by experiencing its personal usefulness and necessity. Thus with the beginning of the age of reason Emile would be able to make a choice not on the basis of belief but after consideration of necessity and usefulness. The acceptance of a government, for instance, would not be a product of youthful indoctrination or the establishment of a fixed set of beliefs but a choice resulting from a process of reasoning.

At adolescence, Rousseau argued, the individual was reborn. The development of sexual drives forced the individual out of a narrowly defined sense of self into the social world. The development of moral and social reasoning was a direct outgrowth of self-love. An individual's understanding of others was based on the ability to identify with the feelings of others. Concerns about good and bad with regard to others were to be a result of the identity one established between self and others. At this stage Emile was introduced into society and underwent social and religious education. From this Emile learned that if the authority of individuals and the prejudices of society are eliminated from education, and the individual is educated according to nature, the light of reason becomes the guide for individual action.

At the end of Emile's education he was asked what he had learned. He replied that he had been taught to be free by learning to yield to necessity, the ultimate necessity of life being death. Rather than struggle with destiny, freedom requires its acceptance. He also argued that people cannot obtain freedom under the safeguard of laws. Liberty, he claimed, was not to be found in government but in the heart of the free person.

ONE OF THE SIGNIFICANT FAILURES of *Emile* was Rousseau's plan for making all social and moral beliefs the product of reasoning based on necessity and usefulness. It was the nineteenth-century anarchist Max Stirner who developed this idea to its fullest and labeled it the ownership of self. Stirner, whose real name was Johann

Casper Schmidt, was a poor German schoolteacher who during the 1840's attended meetings of the Young Hegelians in Berlin with Karl Marx and Friedrich Engels. In 1842 Marx published Stirner's important article on education, "The False Principle of Our Education," in the *Rheinische Zeitung*. In 1844 Stirner completed his book *The Ego and His Own* which so upset Marx that he later devoted a large section of *The German Ideology* to an attack on Stirner.[3]

Stirner essentially agreed with Rousseau that the method of education should allow for individual choice of belief. He premised this on the idea that individuals should at all times make their knowledge and beliefs subservient to their own needs and desires. In a sense the real test of this was their ability to *rid* themselves of any particular idea and belief. As Stirner wrote in his book, *The Ego and His Own*, "The thought is my own only when I have no misgiving about bringing it in danger of death every moment, when I do not have to fear its loss as a loss for me, a loss of me."[4] The thought that one could *not* get rid of, the thought which *owned* the individual, was what Stirner referred to as the "wheel in the head"—the moral imperative which told one what should be done. It was the thought which controlled the will, the knowledge which used the individual, rather than being used by the individual.

For Stirner the ownership of self meant the elimination of "wheels in the head." This was a theme he elaborated on in "The False Principle of Our Education." Stirner made a distinction between a "freeman" and an "educated man." For the educated man knowledge was used to shape character; it became a wheel in the head which allowed him to be possessed by the church, state or humanity. For the freeman knowledge was used to facilitate choice. "If one awakens in men the idea of freedom," Stirner wrote,

> then the freemen will incessantly go on to free themselves; if, on the contrary, one only educates

them, then they will at all times accommodate themselves to circumstances in the most highly educated and elegant manner and degenerate into subservient cringing souls.[5]

For the freeman knowing something was the source of greater choice, while for the educated man knowing something was the *determiner* of choice.

The major problem with modern society, Stirner believed, was that it was full of educated people instead of free people. "Man," Stirner warned, "your head is haunted; you have wheels in your head! ... An idea that has subjected the man to itself." The problem was how to achieve not political liberty but ownership of self. Stirner objected to the idea of political liberty because it only meant the freedom of institutions and ideology. "Political liberty," he wrote,

> meant that the polis, the State, is free; freedom of religion that religion is free, as freedom of conscience signifies that conscience is free; not, therefore, that I am free from the State, from religion, from conscience, or that I am rid of them.[6]

This made the control and nature of education the central issue for modern society.

The real source of power in a society was the institution which owned the inner life of the individual. In the past the church fulfilled the mission of guiding and dominating the mind. In the world of the nineteenth century the dominating influence was becoming the politics of the state. Religion and politics gained power by their ability to establish imperatives directing the actions of the individual. Stirner wrote, "Under religion and politics man finds himself at the standpoint of *should*: he should become this and that, should be so and so. With this postulate, this commandment, every one steps not only in front of another but also in front of himself."[7]

The power of the modern state lay in its recognition of the importance of domination of the mind. In the modern state, laws were internalized within the individual, so that "freedom" merely meant the freedom to obey the laws that one had been taught to believe. It was the dream of the nineteenth-century schoolmasters to end disobedience through the internalization of law in the public schools. Stirner wrote, in one of his finest passages,

> Here at last the domination of the law is for the first time complete. "Not I live, but the law lives in me." Thus I have really come so far to be only the vessel of its glory. Every Prussian carries his gendarme in his breast, says a high Prussian officer.

Placing the gendarme in the breast was the goal of the modern state. Freedom meant freedom from direct control of the state and freedom to act according to the laws of the state. Stirner quoted François Guizot, an important political leader in France in the 1840's, as stating, "The great difficulty of to-day is the guiding and dominating of the mind. Formerly the church fulfilled this mission; now it is not adequate to it. It is from the university that this great service must be expected. . . ." It was for this reason, Guizot argued, that government had the duty of supporting the university. Stirner pointed out that the charter being issued for the university called for freedom of thought and conscience. He quietly commented, "So, in favor of freedom of thought and conscience, the minister demands 'the guiding and dominating of the mind.' "[8]

Domination was not only an internalization of a concrete ideology which had direct and immediate reference to the needs of a society. Domination also referred to the ideal, the moral imperative that captured the loyalty of the individual. There were two levels of wheels in the head. The first level led people through everyday life. One went to church and paid taxes because that was what one was taught; that was the way one lived. On the second level were *ideals*—ideals that drove people to sacrifice themselves for the good of the fatherland, that made them try to be Christ-like, ideals that led them to give up what they were for some unrealizable goal. It was this realm of ideals upon which the strength of the church and state was built. Patriotism and religious fervor were the results of people being possessed by ideals.

The ideal gains possession of people, Stirner argued, because of a confusion between what is *thinkable* and what is *possible*. Just because one can think that all people can be good does not mean that it is possible for all people to be good nor that they ought to be good. Yet it is precisely this "sleight of mind," Stirner suggested, that occurs. "It was thinkable that men might become rational; thinkable, that they might know Christ; thinkable, that they might become moral . . . that they might be obedient subjects . . ." Since it was thinkable, it was possible, "and further, because it was possible to men . . . therefore they ought to be so, it was their calling; and finally—one is to take men only according to this calling, only as called men, 'not as they are, but as they ought to be.' " From this point of view, individuals in the modern world were driven creatures who sacrificed what they were for some ideal of what they ought to be. People did not own themselves but were owned by what they ought to be. The church told people they ought to be like Christ, the state that they ought to be good citizens, and the liberal politician that they ought to give all to the cause of humanity. Modern individuals could never find themselves because of a world surrounded with images of what they ought to be. "Man is not the individual," Stirner wrote, "but man is a thought, an ideal, to which the individual is related not even as the child to the man, but as a chalk point to a point thought of . . ." Both the possibility and moral imperativeness of an ideal gain existence because they too can be formulated by thought. The thought of the dominant institutions became the moral imperative of a society. In the past the dominant institution was the church with its handmaiden, the priest; in the nineteenth century it was the state and its preacher, the schoolmaster. "Thus," Stirner wrote, "the thinkers rule in the world as long as the age of priests or of schoolmasters lasts, and what they think of is possible, but what is possible must be realized."[9]

Stirner believed that for individuals to own themselves they must gain beliefs not through schooling but through actions of the will. In other words, a person might find it *useful* to believe in something and act according to that belief. All ideas and actions were to be judged in terms of their value to the person. The distinction Stirner made was essentially the difference between learning a religious catechism at an early age and making a choice later in life about joining a church. On the one hand, learning to believe in a religion at an early age put a wheel in the head that was difficult to lose. Religion becomes, as Stirner stated, "An idea that has subjected the man to itself." On the other hand, if one chose a religion through the exercise of reason based on relevant knowledge and free of any belief about what ought to be, that belief was *owned* by that person. If one owned the thought, one could get rid of it; it did not own the individual.

Of course in the case of religion, Stirner assumed that nobody would want to own such a belief if given a choice. Religion and the state depended upon the teaching of dogma. If people truly owned themselves, Stirner assumed, they would not find religion or the state useful and would not choose them.

Stirner also criticized the idea of equality in the modern state. Equality within the state amounted simply to equal treatment by the state. "As citizens of the State," Stirner wrote, "they are certainly all equal for the State. But it will divide them and advance them or put them in the rear, according to its special ends, if on no other account; and still more must it distinguish them from one another as good and bad citizens." Within the framework of equality and freedom, the modern state turned all things to its own ends. Equality before the law did not mean the end of injustice, for all people could be treated equally under unjust laws.[10]

The belief in the rightness of the state was the main problem. If people became citizens and lived for the state, then the state could sanctify all actions. "If the welfare of the State is the end, war is a hallowed means; if justice is the State's end, homicide is a hallowed means, and is called by its sacred name, 'execution'; the sacred State hallows every thing that is serviceable to it." The state was an instrument of power for the dominant elite in a society. If the elite killed through the state it was justice. If a citizen killed in retaliation, it was a crime. This situation could exist only if people were taught to believe in the concept of the state. Just as the church taught morality for God, schools taught citizenship for the state.

The solution to the problem of the state was a direct outgrowth of Stirner's reflections on education—knowledge would become a vehicle for self-ownership, a tool by which people made choices about what was useful to them. Stirner envisioned replacing the state with a Union of Egoists—a social organization of free individuals in which there would be no sacrifice to meaningless abstraction; like the "welfare of human society." Social organizations and institutions would be based on the needs of each individual. When their usefulness ended, so would the institutions.[11]

Stirner never stated in any detail how one would achieve an education free of dogma and moral imperatives or how an individual could be freed of the wheels in the head. This process became a goal for libertarian educators. They often got bogged down in circular arguments about a non-dogmatic education itself establishing its own dogma. Some radicals found themselves in the strange position of taking a strong ideological stance toward social problems but fearing to convey that belief to the child. For example, the American anarchist Emma Goldman warned radical parents at the beginning of the twentieth century that if they imposed beliefs on their children, they would find that the

> boy or girl, over-fed on Thomas Paine, will land in the arms of the Church, or they will vote for imperialism only to escape the drag of economic determinism and scientific socialism, or that they ... cling to their right of accumulating property, only to find relief from the old-fashioned communism of their father.[12]

THE DILEMMA OF ESTABLISHING an education for self-ownership was highlighted in Francisco Ferrer's Modern School in Spain. When Ferrer set about organizing his school in the 1890's, he searched for non-dogmatic books for its library. He found himself completely frustrated in his search and consequently the school opened without a single volume in its library.[13] The inability to find a non-dogmatic text illustrates the danger of libertarian education becoming a vacuum, with adults fearing to pass on *any* knowledge. This extreme was never reached in the nineteenth century because of a basic belief in the objective facts of science and human reason. There was an overriding faith that there existed a body of objective natural and social laws that people could learn and use for their own benefit.

It was within the framework of science and rationalism that Ferrer tried to actualize an education for self-ownership and freedom from dogmatic control. He believed the role of the teacher to be that of planting the germ of ideas which would grow within the range of the individual's reason. The germ of the ideas was to be in the form of the exact sciences. "The work of man's cerebral energy is to create the ideal," Ferrer wrote, "with the aid of art and philosophy. But in order that the ideal shall not degenerate into fables, or mystic and unsubstantial dreams . . . it is absolutely necessary to give it a secure and unshakable foundation in the exact sciences."[14]

The only purpose in teaching the exact sciences was to provide a basis for the use of reason. Education was not designed to make a person into a good citizen, a religious person, or even a good person. Any such goal was viewed as dogmatic, as imposing an ideal of what ought to be. It was for this reason that there were no rewards or punishments in Ferrer's Modern School. "Since we are not educating for a specific purpose," Ferrer wrote, "we cannot determine the capacity or incapacity of the child." In other words, in an educational process with no particular goal or end, the children could not be rewarded or punished because there was nothing to be punished for.[15]

There were goals, of course. Whether these goals defeated the idea of non-dogmatic education was a question that provided endless debate in libertarian circles and proved utterly unanswerable. Ferrer clearly stated,

> It must be the aim of the rational schools to show the children that there will be tyranny and slavery as long as one man depends upon another, to study the causes of the prevailing ignorance, to learn the origin of all the traditional practices which give life to the existing social system, and to direct the attention of the pupils to these matters.

One feels confident that Ferrer would have dismissed any criticism of this goal as nonsense. He was convinced that there was an objective set of facts that could be learned without subjecting the student to an ideology.

One example was Ferrer's technique of teaching arithmetic. This was discussed earlier in this chapter as an illustration of either enslavement or freedom through knowledge. Ferrer wanted arithmetic taught with examples dealing with the just distribution of production, communication, transportation, the benefits of machinery, and public works. "In a word," Ferrer wrote, "the Modern School wants a number of problems showing what arithmetic really ought to be—the science of the social economy (taking the work economy in its etymological sense of 'good distribution')."[16] In this sense objective fact or knowledge had a special meaning. It was objective in the sense that individuals could use it for maintaining their own individual freedom. Arithmetic placed in the framework of the existing economic systems became a method by which individuals were indoctrinated into those systems. On the other hand, arithmetic presented as a tool for creating a more just organization of the economy was knowledge that individuals could use to free themselves.

Another example of this type of method was Emma Goldman's criticism of traditional methods of teaching history. She wrote, "See how the events of the world become like a cheap puppet show, where a few wire-pullers are supposed to have directed the course of development of the entire race." History which emphasized the actions of rulers, governments, and great men conditioned the individual to accept a society in which most people were expected to be passive with a few leaders directing events. Emma Goldman believed history should emphasize the ability of all people to act and shape the direction of history. History presented in the traditional manner enslaved humanity to authoritarian institutions. But when history is portrayed with all people as active agents, individuals learn of their power to shape the future.[17]

The educational process in these examples loses its dogmatism and moral direction—it presents material the individual can use to obtain freedom. The problem with this technique is that it skirts the issue of how the individual can learn about a particular ideology out of a desire to understand. How does one learn about religion without becoming religious? How does one learn about capitalism without becoming a capitalist? Should one in fact isolate the child from all beliefs? Couldn't one learn more about the real meaning of an ideology by listening to a believer argue his or her cause?

ONE WAY OUT of this particular dilemma was offered by the Christian anarchist and Russian novelist, Leo Tolstoy, who established a school in Russia in the 1860's. Tolstoy resolved the issue by replacing the concept of education with that of *culture*. He argued that one had to make a clear distinction between the concepts of culture, education, instruction, and teaching. Culture was defined as the total of all the social forces which shaped the character of the individual. Education was the conscious attempt to give people a particular type of character and habit. As Tolstoy stated, "Education is the tendency of one man to make another just like himself." The difference between education and culture was *compulsion*. "Education is culture under restraint. Culture is free." Tolstoy argued that instruction and teaching were related to both education and culture. Instruction was the transmission of one person's information to another; teaching was the instruction of physical skills. Teaching and instruction were means of culture, Tolstoy claimed, when they were free. They were means of education, "when the teaching is forced upon the pupil, and when the instruction is exclusive, that is when only those subjects are taught which the educator regards as necessary."[18]

Learning, then, should be a process of culture and not of education. The school should practice non-interference, with students left free to learn what they wanted to learn. Tolstoy defined a school as "the conscious activity of he who gives culture upon those who receive it . . ." Non-interference in the school meant "granting the person . . . the full freedom to avail himself of the teaching which answers his need, which he wants . . . and to avoid teaching which he does not need and which he does not want." Museums and public lectures were examples of schools of non-interference: they were consciously planned to achieve a certain goal, but the user was free to attend or not to attend. Established schools and universities, on the other hand, used a system of rewards and punishments and limited the area of studies to achieve their particular ends. A non-compulsory school was one without a planned program where teachers could teach what they wanted and their offerings would be regulated by the demands of the students. The school would not be interested in how its teaching was used or what the effect would be on the students. The school would be a place of culture and not of education.

Tolstoy's solution essentially tried to solve the Stirner-ian problem of self-ownership by eliminating all compulsory institutions that were designed to turn a person *into* something. This was premised on a profound belief that if people were allowed to be self-regulating, they would choose the best and most rewarding life. For Tolstoy, who was a Christian anarchist, self-regulation meant allowing people to be governed by the goodness of God within themselves. This, of course, was a concept rejected by strict rationalists like Ferrer and anti-religious thinkers like Stirner. Yet if the religious argument is overlooked, there are possible grounds for agreement between Stirner and Tolstoy on the issue of self-regulation, centering on the relationship between teacher and student. Both Stirner and Tolstoy would probably have agreed that self-regulation is impossible as long as the traditional teacher-student relationship exists and the school continues consciously to plan a particular outcome.

STIRNER'S ANALYSIS of the relationship between student and teacher was one of his most profound contributions to the understanding of the enslavement of humanity in the modern world. Ownership of self was more than just a matter of not forcing moral imperatives and dogma on the individual; it was also a matter of free exercise of the will. The very existence of a teacher-to-student relationship froze the will of the individual. In fact this relationship prepared individuals to give up their wills to the authority of social institutions.

Stirner believed that knowledge which was *taught* turned individuals into learners rather than creative persons. Learners lost their freedom of will through increasing dependency on experts and institutions for instructions on how to act. They were without free will because they depended on *learning* how to act rather than *determining* for themselves how to act.

> Where will a creative person be educated instead of a learning one, where does the teacher turn into a fellow worker, where does he recognize knowledge as turning into will, where does the *free man* count as a goal and not the merely *educated*? [emphasis added] [19]

To avoid turning people into mere learners, the goal of pedagogy should be self-development—in the sense of an individual gaining self-awareness and the ability to act. The existing schools worked against the freedom of the will.

In discussing the development of education up to his time, Stirner argued that following the Reformation, education in the humanistic tradition was a source of power: ". . . . education, as a power, raised him who possessed it over the weak, who lacked it, and the educated man counted . . . as the mighty, the powerful, the imposing one: for he was an authority." The rise of the idea of universal schooling, on the other hand, undermined the authority of the humanist scholar with a new system designed to produce citizens trained for practical life. Authority in the system of popular education was not that of one person over another; it was the authority of the dogma of the practical and useful. This new educational authority meant not subservience to the scholar, but subservience to an ideology of pragmatism. Neither idea was to Stirner's liking, ". . . only scholars come out of the menageries of the humanists, only 'useful citizens' out of those of the realists, both of whom are indeed nothing but subservient people." Education for practical life, Stirner believed, produced people of principle who acted according to maxims. "Most college students," he stated, "are living examples of this sad turn of events. Trained in the most excellent manner, they go on in training; drilled, they continue drilling."[20]

In the framework of Stirner's argument the growth of public schools in the nineteenth century takes on added meaning. As we have pointed out, the schools were tied to the idea of turning out useful citizens trained for practical life. The school assumed responsibility for the *whole child*. Individual free will and initiative became subservient to the expertise of the teacher. The enslavement of the individual was the result of the actions of the individual being turned over to the production line of education.

To understand this concept fully one must place it within the broad historical framework of the development of the school. What Stirner was witnessing in the nine-teenth-century school was the steady *institutionalization of the socialization process*. Some form of school had always existed in Western society but its role had been what Tolstoy referred to as instruction and teaching, not education. Schools existed often on a voluntary basis to teach reading, writing, and skills needed for the church or business. Churches, of course, developed schools for their own moral purposes. Most of the ways an individual learned how to act were a part of growing and living within the family and community. There was little separation between the socialization process and the world in which individuals acted out their lives. Willing and acting were a part of life and one saw one's actions as a product of one's interactions with society.

The school was fast becoming the *central agency* for socialization, though. It was assuming more and more responsibility for completely educating or shaping the individual. Socialization became more a product of the life of the school than of the life of the community. By the end of the nineteenth century, educators like John Dewey were expressing concern about this situation, demanding that the school become a community that reflected the real life of the surrounding world. From the viewpoint of educators like Dewey the school had to be *accepted* as the central agency of socialization—the problem was to make it effective by turning it into a real community.

Stirner asserted that within the school knowledge did not grow as part of a process of action and exercise of will, but was taught by a teacher and then acted upon by the student. What the school really taught the individual was how to be a learner. This took Stirner far beyond many other libertarian educators of the nineteenth century. He would have rejected Ferrer, not because Ferrer wanted a non-dogmatic education, but because he wanted a *school*. In Tolstoy's terms, Stirner wanted a society where socialization was a product of culture and not of education. Ownership of self meant freedom from dogma and moral imperatives *and* a will that did not depend on authoritarian sources. Ownership of self meant freedom from schools themselves.

In the twentieth century this theme has been elaborated upon by Ivan Illich. Illich sees the teacher-student relationship as the backbone of the enslavement of modern humanity to a mass consumer society. He argues that what people learn in school is to trust the judgment of the educator and distrust their own judgment. In school one learns proper and socially useful ways of working, studying, using leisure time, and enjoying life. This prepares one to accept a society that provides packages and programs for all aspects of life. The will is frozen until an expert prescribes or approves. Illich wrote in 1971,

> ... in a service centered economy man is estranged from what he can "do" as well as from what he can "make," ... he has delivered his mind and heart over to therapeutic treatment even more completely than he has sold away the fruits of his labor.

For Illich, "Schools have alienated man from his learning." The process of schooling turns the individual completely over to the control and authority of experts and institutions.[2][1]

Explicit in Illich's thinking and implicit in Stirner's is the idea that the only solution would be the creation of a society in which schools would neither exist nor be necessary. This would not mean the end of institutions to pass on skills, but the end of institutions with curriculums designed to make people into something, to manipulate them. Knowledge and learning within such a society would be linked to real-life processes and personal usefulness. Knowledge and learning would not be placed in a special institution.

Implied in the concept of a society without schools is the end of all other institutions which are breeding grounds for dogma and moral imperatives. In a sense the church and state are themselves schools, with ideas of how people should act and what they ought to be. A society without schools would be one without institutions of mysticism and authority. It would be a society of *self-regulation* where institutions would be products of personal need and usefulness and not sources of power.

Certainly Francisco Ferrer might have responded to the idea of deschooling society by saying that one could not *wish* a non-authoritarian society into being and that the Modern School was the beginning of a plan to move in that direction. Stirner never fully dealt with the problem of passing on knowledge without filling the head with wheels and ideals. But he was sure, as Elizabeth Burns Ferm (an American educator and eventually the head of an American-style Modern School) wrote in 1907, that the educator to be avoided was the one that endeavored "to make and leave an impression on the child."[2][2]

IN THE TWENTIETH CENTURY libertarian groups have tried to implement these educational goals, either by creating non-authoritarian schools or by rejecting the concept of schooling altogether. Those who sought to establish libertarian institutions of schooling envisioned learning centers that would avoid the institutionalization of controls.

One of the problems that has confronted contemporary libertarians is that they live in a highly organized and rationalized technological society which leaves little room for the individual to grow and develop through the exercise of individual will. Urban industrial society is already so highly organized that children can find little opportunity to explore and construct their own world. Added to this is the uniformity of the equipment available to educational leaders—mass-produced learning aids and playthings which are used to rationalize the development of the individual. The libertarian tradition requires not

53

only freedom from the imposition of ideology but also freedom for self-development, and the twentieth century has witnessed a wide variety of educational experiments designed to create environments for self-development.

The Modern School movement begun by Ferrer and A.S. Neill's Summerhill represent part of this libertarian concern; in the 1950's and 1960's it was further evidenced in a very widespread movement for the establishment of "free schools" and alternative forms of education. The free school movement was an attempt to establish an environment for self-development in a world that was considered overly structured and rationalized. One of the precursors of the "free school" idea of the 1960's, for instance, was the development of the "free playground" movement in the 1940's. This movement was an expression of libertarian concern about reshaping the world so that people could control and use it for their own purposes.[2 3] The first free playground was begun in Copenhagen in 1943 and shortly after World War II the idea spread to Sweden, Switzerland, and the United States. In Stockholm the playground was known as "Freetown," in Minneapolis as "The Yard," and in Switzerland as "Robinson Crusoe playgrounds." The basic principle of the adventure playground was that it was equipped only with raw material and tools, lumber, nails, junk metal, shovels, and building equipment. There was no manufactured equipment such as swings or see-saws; essentially the children were given the means to build, destroy, and rebuild their playgrounds.[2 4]

The interesting thing about the adventure playground movement is its implicit criticism of a new component of authoritarian control: the urban-industrial *environment* itself, as represented in the highly structured school and playground. Manufactured equipment on the playground tends to structure play itself, and leave little room for creativity or experiment. In this sense a free school or a free playground could provide an opportunity for the child to experience an unstructured environment.

In this context one can understand that libertarian involvement in the free school movement of the 1960's was taking one solution to the problem of education: free schools as an oasis from authoritarian control and as a means of passing on the knowledge to be free. On the surface one could argue that the term "free school" was contradictory. How could a school be free if, as Tolstoy argued, a school was a conscious attempt to turn one into a "something"? The free school movement was, and still is, a very complex phenomenon with roots partly in Freudian and Reichian psychology, as represented in A.S. Neill's Summerhill, and partly in traditional libertarian concerns about authority, as best exemplified in Ferrer and the Modern Schools. Part of the movement can be explained, as we shall see in the chapter on Reich and Neill, in terms of changing psychological perspectives, and part of the movement can be explained in terms of an attempt to provide a free and unstructured environment. George Dennison, one of the popular leaders of the free school movement, wrote in 1966 that his "First Street School is radical and experimental. There are no grades, no graded report cards, no competitive examinations. No child is compelled to study or answer questions when he does not want to."[2 5] At first glance there would appear to be very little that was "radical" about a situation without grades, report cards, or examinations. After all, that is the way things "should" be. But placed in a broader perspective, these changes were radical in the sense that the First Street School represented a refuge from a society that was highly structured and graded and left little room for self-development.

One of the major spokesmen for the free school movement was America's leading libertarian philosopher, Paul Goodman. Goodman wrote not only about schooling but also about the nature and direction of modern society. He was one of the leading spokesmen for the decentralization of urban and technological structures. Concerned with maximizing individual autonomy, he argued for the decentralization of industry to a local level so that the individual could directly control the use of technology. In the same manner he argued for decentralization and democratic local control of bureaucracies.[26]

Goodman continued the libertarian tradition by arguing that schooling had become a process by which the individual was stamped, graded, certified, and returned to society. All of this, he argued, was for the benefit of the ruling industrial elite. He wrote in *Compulsory Mis-Education* in the early 1960's that the real function of education was to grade and market skills. "This means, in effect, that a few great corporations are getting the benefit of an enormous weeding out and selective process—all children are fed into the mill and everybody pays for it."[27] Goodman's plans for education involved the decentralization of large and cumbersome school systems and the establishment of small-scale schools. He offered a plan which together with A.S. Neill's ideas gave direction to the free school movement. Goodman suggested that in some cases schools could dispense with their classes and use streets, stores, museums, movies, and factories as places of learning. The use of certified teachers could be dispensed with and people like the druggist, the storekeeper, and the factory worker could be used as teachers. And, most important, the school would be non-compulsory. Within cities it would be reduced to a mini-school which through decentralization would be influenced by the desires of the students and the neighborhood community.[28]

IT WAS IVAN ILLICH in the late 1960's who gave the libertarian tradition new life both in terms of criticisms and proposals. Illich argues that schools themselves are the problem. They are a source of ideological control, and they reproduce and reinforce the existing social structure. The schools also serve to alienate people from their learning and make them dependent on the authority of institutions and experts. Illich's proposals for deschooling society overcome some of the inherent problems of the free school movement. The free school movement has assumed the need for something called a school to overcome the problems of an existing structured society. The danger lies in the possibility that the free school would become even *more* therapeutic, and create even more *dependency*, than the established school. What individuals might actually learn in such a school was that they needed an institution to give them freedom. Illich rejects the concept of the free school and argues that true autonomy can result only from changes in institutional styles. It is within this context that the deschooling of society is to take place.

Ivan Illich's concept of what education should be is very much like Tolstoy's. In fact, one could argue that he is within this traditional stream of Christian anarchism. Both Illich and Tolstoy want people to have the chance to experience culture without the creation of an institution called the school which tries consciously to turn people into something, to shape people according to a preconceived goal, by means of an organized curriculum.

The most pressing problem of the modern world, Illich argues, is to change the style of institutions and technology so that they work for the benefit of the individual. A series of "public utilities" for education which people could use for their own purposes would serve this goal. These utilities would be organized so that no one could gain a position of power in them. Essentially what Illich proposes is dividing the functions of schooling into separate and distinct units. For instance, he suggests a public utility that would be an information center, a kind of expanded library where books and other media would be available, as well as information on such things as visiting industrial centers and on opportunities to observe a variety of community activities. Another distinct utility would be a place where people could register their skills—typing, fishing, bricklaying, knowledge of history, etc. Those who wished to learn a skill could then find someone who had that skill and was willing to teach it. At both the information center and the skill center individuals would be free to choose whatever information or skills they wanted to learn. There would be no one in a position to make those decisions for the individual nor decide what was in the individual's best interest. The divorce of the two functions would avoid the possibility of the development of an extended and graded curriculum. There might be a curriculum *within* a skill like typing, but this curriculum would not extend beyond that particular skill. In other words, the curriculum planning would be completely turned over to the individual. Illich also proposes another utility or communications system as a means of linking people of common interests. This could be either computer matching, journals dealing with specific interests, or simple notices in which people would register the interests that they wished to share.[29]

Illich's exploration of differing institutional styles expresses traditional libertarian interests more consistently than the free schools, which served as oases of free activity but failed to effect any change in the overall structure of society. They were schools with planned purposes and as such always stood the chance of being used as institutions of control. Illich's plans emphasize the separation of learning and control. In the eighteenth and nineteenth centuries, William Godwin, Max Stirner, Leo Tolstoy, and other anarchists recognized this as one of the fundamental problems for modern society. In the twentieth century, with the expansion of schooling and psychological techniques of control within the school, the problem has become even more pressing. As Max Stirner argues, people must control the learning processes by which they grow before they can truly own themselves. It is this goal of control over the learning process that contemporary libertarian educationists such as Goodman, Illich and others have continued to explore.

Arnold Jacobi

3
THE GROWTH OF CONSCIOUSNESS: MARX TO FREIRE

KARL MARX REFERRED to Max Stirner as a man in revolt against the "rule of thoughts," who believed that if you taught people "to knock them out of their heads . . . existing reality . . . would collapse."[1] This, Marx said, was very much like believing that drowning resulted from people being possessed with the idea of gravity; if you knocked the idea out of their heads by showing it to be a superstition or a religious idea, it "would be proof against any danger from water." It was not enough to talk about the "spooks" controlling human consciousness without talking about the social reality which produced those spooks. This link between social reality and consciousness had important implications for pedagogical methods, becoming a key element in the educational proposals of twentieth-century humanist psychologists like Carl Rogers and in the pedagogical techniques of the Brazilian educator Paulo Freire.

Paulo Freire, in conducting literacy programs for adults in Brazil in the mid-twentieth century, developed a perspective which combined educational methods with this Marxian concept of consciousness. The separation of thought and action is overcome by linking learning to will and social action. Learning becomes an instrument for individual liberation. Freire first set forth his educational method in his doctoral dissertation at the University of Recife in Brazil in 1959. While working as Professor of History and Philosophy of Education at the same university, his teaching methods were implemented throughout the northeastern part of Brazil. After the military coup of 1964, Freire was jailed by the government for his educational activities. He was "invited" to leave the country and spent the next five years working in Chile, then became a consultant at Harvard University. Freire's lectures at Ivan Illich's Center for Intercultural Documentation in Mexico in 1970 and 1971 attracted students from throughout South America. In Mexico and other Latin American countries his techniques have been implemented in both rural and urban settings. Freire must be considered one of the most important educational philosophers of the twentieth century.

At the heart of Freire's educational method is a concept of humanity which owes its origin to Marx's concern with the development of individual consciousness and alienation in modern society. His concept of human potential in many ways fulfills the meaning of consciousness as defined by Marx and gives expression to Stirner's concept of ownership of self. One must understand Freire's concept of humanity in order to grasp his educational method. Freire's whole technique stands in danger of being trivialized unless this concept is emphasized.

The goal of social life, Freire argues, is the humanization of the world. By this he means a process by which each person becomes conscious of the social forces working upon him or her, reflects upon those forces, and becomes capable of transforming the world. To be human is to be an actor who makes choices and seeks to guide one's own destiny. To be free, to be an actor, means knowing who one is and how one has been shaped by the surrounding social world. It is one's social world and environment that determine the nature of one's consciousness and ideology. Without a knowledge and awareness of that determination, humanization is impossible.

The opposite of a humanized world, in Freire's terms, a dehumanized world, is one without self-awareness, without a consciousness of the historical forces determining existence. Without this consciousness people are unable to become actors in the stream of history and are simply *acted upon* by history. This condition of oppression is what Freire calls the *culture of silence*. The culture of silence can be a product either of simple ignorance or of education itself. By being kept in a state of simple ignorance, the peasant in Brazil can be locked in this culture of silence, never realizing the forces that caused his or her poverty. On the other hand, an educational program which only assimilates the peasant into the very social system which caused impoverishment in the first place, is not a liberatory force. Freire would have agreed with Stirner that education can produce wheels in the head that stand in the way of consciousness of self.

This concept of humanization implies, as Marx stated, that "consciousness can never be anything else than conscious existence, and the existence of men is their actual life-process." In a pedagogical sense this means that to expand consciousness is to make one aware of one's life processes. From Marx's standpoint, however, life was not determined by consciousness but consciousness by life, and it was this criticism that he leveled at Stirner. The interaction of an individual with the world determined his or her subjective view of the world and of self. In other words, an individual learned a concept of self, whom he or she was, by the nature of his or her relationships to society. Human interaction with the world also produced an ideology and an understanding of the world. As Marx wrote, "We set out from real, active men, and on the basis of their real life-process we demonstrate the development of the ideological reflexes and echoes of this life-process."[2]

For Freire, to know the objective world is to begin to know oneself. If learning is to be meaningful, it must be tied to the life process of the individual. Freire's method of teaching illiterates began with a concrete study of the everyday lives of the people. For example, in a small village a team of educators would work in cooperation with the villagers to develop thematic representations of the life processes of the residents. These would then be presented to the villagers in the form of pictures, tapes, or any appropriate media. The thematic representations would contain certain problems and contradictions in the culture which could serve as the basis for discussion. In Freire's words,

> Utilizing certain basic contradictions, we must pose this existential, concrete, present situation to the people as a problem which challenges them and requires a response—not just at the intellectual level, but at the level of action.[3]

One example presented a scene of a drunken man walking on a street and three men standing on a corner talking. This scene was shown to a group of tenement dwellers in Santiago to raise questions about the causal relationships within their particular social organization and culture.[4] The discussions resulting from such thematic representations would be the source for the words that would form the basis of the literacy campaign.

Language is tied directly to the life processes of the learner and thus becomes a source of self-understanding. As individuals progress in reading and writing by using

64

words that help them understand their world, their awareness of self constantly expands. For Freire, acquiring literacy through thematic representations becomes a means of *objectifying* the individual's world. It gives the individual the necessary tools for thinking about the world. A culture of silence is one in which people are unable to distance themselves from their life activity, making it impossible for them to rise to the level of reflection. The dialogue around thematic representations provides a means toward reflection and a basis for both literacy and self-consciousness.

Within this framework learning becomes a source of liberation and a tool for social change. People are dehumanized because they lack a full awareness of their life activity. This is why people in a culture of silence do nothing to change their world. Freire agrees with Marx that "the animal is one with its life activity. It does not distinguish the activity from itself. It is its activity."[5] In this sense, those in a culture of silence remain at a level of mere animal activity; in fact, the source of economic and political oppression is precisely the reduction of human beings to this state. Freire wants to restore humanity to the oppressed by giving them a conscious life. As Marx wrote, "But man makes his life itself an object of his will and consciousness. He has a conscious life activity. . . . Conscious life activity distinguishes man from the life activity of animals."[6]

For Marx, Freire, and the twentieth-century existentialist psychologists, it is in the realm of consciousness that the contradiction between freedom and determinism is overcome. While consciousness and life activity are determined by material conditions, a person who has no consciousness of self, who has nothing but life activity, is completely propelled by social forces. But the person who is *aware* of these forces and *conscious* of their nature is able to break with the trajectory of history and participate in the radical change of self and society. Rollo May, writing about existential psychology in the mid-twentieth century, argues that while psychology must recognize deterministic factors and human finiteness,

> In the revealing and exploring of these deterministic forces in the patient's life, the patient is orienting himself in some particular way to the data and thus is engaged in some choice, no matter how seemingly insignificant; is experiencing some freedom, no matter how subtle.[7]

And it is precisely toward this relationship to the individual's world that Freire's educational method is meant to lead.

In this method the tying of language and learning to the life processes is meant to overcome the separation of thought and action. The dialogue based on thematic representations of everyday life is meant to grow into a greater consciousness of the surrounding social reality. Theory and activity are to be brought together in social action. According to Freire, ". . . a revolution is achieved with neither verbalism nor activism, but rather with praxis, that is, with reflection and action directed at the structures to be transformed." A drawing of tenement living conditions might be presented to the poor of an area and from this would grow a reflective process questioning the conditions and their social causes. No theory as to *why* the conditions existed would be given to the poor; rather, theory would be a product of the reflection and action of the people themselves.

> The leaders cannot treat the oppressed as mere activists to be denied the opportunity of reflection and allowed merely the illusion of acting. . . . It is absolutely essential that the oppressed participate in the revolutionary process with an increasingly critical awareness of their role as subjects of the transformation.[8]

This praxis would end the separation of thought and action that Marx had argued was contributing to human fragmentation and alienation. The origins of this separation, according to Marx's interpretation, lay in the historical development of the separation of classes and the division of labor. The separation of manual and mental labor in the development of civilization permitted the separation of consciousness from life activity. Marx wrote in *The German Ideology* that with the division between mental and manual labor

> consciousness can really flatter itself that it is something other than consciousness of existing practice, that it is really conceiving something without conceiving something *real*; from now on consciousness is in a position to emancipate itself from the world and to proceed to the formation of "pure" theory, theology, philosophy, ethics, etc.[9]

Marx also saw this division between theory and practice as resulting from the organization of modern industry. In *Capital* he argued that the worker became a mere appendage of the machine, trapped in a life of endless drudgery and routine. Intellectual and reflective powers were not brought into use in manual labor. Marx wrote,

> The separation of the intellectual powers of production from the manual labour, and the conversion of those powers into the might of capital over labour, is, as we have already shown, finally completed by modern industry erected on the foundation of machinery.

People in the modern factory organization were forced into specialized and limited roles with the intellectual activity a function of the managers and owners. Individual skill and worth, Marx argued, "vanishes as an infinitesimal quantity before the science, the gigantic physical forces, and the mass of labour that are embodied in the factory mechanism. . . ."[10]

Separation of thought and action means that theory becomes a product of a class which is separated from life activity. It means that individuals experience a fragmentation of their powers, becoming appendages of the machine rather than giving it control or direction. John Dewey, for instance, wrote in *Education and Democracy* that the separation of liberal education from industrial and professional education was a result "of a division of classes into those who had to labor for a living and those who were relieved from this necessity." Workers, he arued, had no insight into the social aims of their work and, consequently, the "results actually achieved are not the ends of their actions, but only of their employers."[11]

FREIRE ARGUES THAT traditional education was premised on what he calls the "banking" method of education—the idea that a student is an *object* into which knowledge is placed, not a *subject* in the learning process. This banking method of education, Freire argues, shares many of the properties of an oppressive society: "the teacher teaches and the students are taught"; "the teacher thinks and the students are thought about"; "the teacher acts and the students have the illusion of acting through the action of the teacher"; and "the teacher is the subject of the learning process, while the pupils are mere objects."[12] In adult literacy programs the banking theory manifests itself in the use of reading material which has little relationship to the life activity of the learner. Rather, such programs attempt to work upon and change the learner.

The fact that the banking theory turns the learner into an object reflects the assumption that the fundamental problem is not with society but with the individual. In other words, in the case of poverty a banking system of education assumes poverty exists because the poor do not know how to function properly within society. The goal of education, then, is to change the behavior of the poor so that it conforms to the needs of a society which created poverty in the first place. In the very process of educating the poor, all blame is placed upon them. They are condemned, essentially by being told they have failed.

In this manner the consciousness of the oppressed is changed without changing the oppressive conditions of society. Education as banking is not liberating but contributes to the docility and alienation of the oppressed. Marx's concept of alienation illuminates the full meaning of Freire's criticism of the banking method. For Marx, work should function to objectify the self and hence provide the individual with a source of *self-awareness*. Work or activity that becomes foreign to or alienated from the individual—as it does in the case of the banking method of education—does not fulfill this function. In answer to the question of what constitutes the alienation of labor, Marx wrote: "First, that the work is external to the worker, that it is not part of his nature; and that, consequently, he does not fulfill himself in his work but denies himself. . . ."[13] In the same manner the learning material of the banking method stands in opposition to the learner. Instead of affirming the learner's life and providing tools for greater understanding, it denies that life and obscures self-awareness.

Within this framework Marx's concept of human alienation is very similar to Freire's concept of the human being as the object of teaching. For Marx alienation meant that work or life activity is not an object for individual fulfillment; rather, the individual becomes a mere object used for production. "The alienation of the worker in his product," he wrote, "means not only that his labor becomes an object, assumes an external existence, but that it exists independently, outside himself, and alien to him, and that it stands opposed to him as an autonomous power."[14]

69

Similarly, in the banking method of education the learner's self becomes an object of the educational process, worked upon to achieve goals external to itself. The goals and content of this kind of education are not a product of the learner, they are not subject to his or her control. The learner is viewed as an object, a means for achieving the teacher's end. The object of teaching is not to understand the self but to change the individual in accordance with alien goals. For instance, the banking method of education not only tells the poor *they* are the *problem*, but also establishes a model of what they should be which is alien to what they are.

The model presented to the oppressed of what they should be like is a model shaped by the oppressor. Such a model inherently tends to perpetuate the existing social structure. Thus both the content and moral imperatives of the banking method reflect the ideology of the ruling class. As Marx wrote, "The ideas of the ruling class are in every epoch the ruling ideas: i.e., the class, which is the ruling material force of society, is at the same time its ruling intellectual force."[15]

What the banking method of education achieves is the creation of a consciousness which is alien to the learner. The poor are given a model based on the life and actions of the rich. Such models were just what Stirner had criticized as moral imperatives which force people to act in contradiction to their own needs and liberation.

ONE OF THE GOALS of Freire's method is to bring those in a culture of silence to an understanding of self which would allow them to expel the internalized image of the dominant class.

> ... when the dominated classes reproduce the dom-
> inators' style of life, it is because the dominators live
> "within" the dominated. The dominated can eject the
> dominators only by getting distance from them and
> objectifying them. Only then can they recognize
> them as their antitheses.[16]

For example, this was precisely the situation confronted
by black people in the United States in their relationship
to white society. By internalizing the style of life of the
white population they were internalizing the very culture
which had been responsible for slavery and racial segrega-
tion. For instance, black people discovered that they had
adopted the same standards of beauty—fair skin and
Caucasian facial features—as white members of the society.
The slogan "Black is Beautiful" represented the beginning
of the ejection of this false consciousness.

Freire's method is thus directed both at the expansion
of consciousness and at the ejection of the false consciousness created by the structure of society. In this sense he
combines the traditional Marxist concern about overcoming alienation with the traditional libertarian desire for
freedom from imposed moral imperatives. This means that
peasants in Latin America must be given the tools to lift
themselves out of the culture of silence and gain conscious
control over the social forces affecting their lives. People
must be helped to see that part of the problem is their own
acceptance of "success" as it has been defined for them by
the dominant class. They must begin to treat their own
lives as *authentic* and not to reject their own realities on
the basis of the values of the dominant class.

Without the ejection of these values, social change
would mean only that one oppressive faction takes the
place of another—essentially a change in palace guard
without any change in the palace. This would not meet the
criteria of a humanistic revolution, which can only be
accomplished through individual liberation of consciousness, through the participation of all people in social
change.

THE RADICALISM OF FREIRE'S PRAXIS, which ties together reflection and action, can be more fully appreciated if it is compared to the ideas of a humanist psychologist like Carl Rogers. Rogers' therapy, and what he calls student-centered teaching, is based on a concept of self-actualization and self-awareness very similar to Freire's ideas. The drive for self-actualization is what Freire calls the "humanism of man (*sic*)"; it is a desire to gain greater conscious control over one's environment. Rogers writes that self-actualization means movement "in the direction of greater independence or self-responsibility . . . in the direction of increasing self-government, self-regulation, and autonomy, and away from heteronymous control, or control by external forces."[17] Self-actualization is achieved through what Rogers calls congruence of the personality. "We may say," he writes, "that freedom from inner tension, or psychological adjustment, exists when the concept of self is at least roughly congruent with all the experiences of the organism."[18] In other words, psychological adjustment occurs when one's concept of self corresponds to the forces that have shaped that self. Congruence of personality means that one has an awareness of the social forces shaping personality and an ability to control and give direction to those forces.

But humanist psychologists like Rogers fail to relate personality to the structure of society and to go beyond self-actualization to the transformation of society. It is after all the organization of society which assumes a major share of the responsibility for non-congruence and lack of self-actualization. The failure to analyze social and political implications is what makes humanist psychology superficial. It is more of a technique for management and adjustment than for changing society. This is one reason why methods like those of Carl Rogers have become popular among school leaders in the United States.

72

These limitations become apparent when humanist psychologists talk about social change. For Carl Rogers the key to social change is a self-actualized person who creates a climate which allows for self-actualization of other people. Rogers calls this the "chain reaction" effect of client-centered therapy.

> Here is a theoretical basis for sound interpersonal, intergroup, and *international relationships*. . . . This atmosphere of understanding and acceptance is the very climate most likely to create a therapeutic experience and consequent self-acceptance in the person who is exposed to it.

For Rogers it is the "psychological 'chain reaction' which appears to have tremendous potentialities for the handling of problems of social relationships."[19] This is a utopian vision which is to grow from the warm acceptance of all people. Compared to Freire's humanized individual engaged in changing self and the world, Rogers' self-actualized person appears incomplete.

The political and social implications of Freire's method become evident in his demonstration of the relationship between levels of individual consciousness and levels of development of political and social organization. Individual liberation through education is closely tied to stages of social liberation. This relationship clearly is not the same as Rogers' "chain reaction" of acceptance, but is rather a process of turning the individual's learning into self-liberation by working to create a liberated society.

Another important point about Freire's attempt to link levels of conscious development to political and social reality is that it makes his educational theory universal, establishing its relevance for highly industrialized societies as well as for those of the Third World.

In Freire's model the lowest level of consciousness is, of course, the culture of silence in the peasant societies of the Third World. In Latin America this takes the form of a rural/urban split, with the rural areas dominated by and dependent on the ruling elites of the urban centers. As stated above, the dependent society accepts the values and life style of the dominator and cannot achieve self-awareness. "This results," Freire writes,

> in the duality of the dependent society, its ambiguity, its being and not being itself, and the ambivalence characteristic of its long experience of dependency, both attracted by and rejecting the metropolitan society.[20]

Individuals at this level of consciousness tend to ascribe the cause of their plight to self-blame or to supernatural sources. For example, peasants might feel that hunger is caused by their own incapacity or that it represents the anger of the gods. In Freire's educational process dialogue about problem situations might at first tend to resort to such explanations, but part of the goal of dialogue would be to aid in going beyond that level of consciousness. The culture of silence also exists in industrial countries. Minority groups in the United States, for example, have only recently been emerging from their own state of dependence, throwing off their self-concepts of natural incapacity and their internalization of the values and life style of the dominator.

Freire's next stage of consciousness and social development is very close to the level of development of most industrial countries. He calls this stage naive-transitiveness because it refers to the beginning of a popular consciousness, one which has not fully emerged from the culture of silence. At this stage pressure and criticism begin to be applied to the dominant groups in the society. The leaders of a society might respond to this by allowing superficial changes and granting certain political and economic privileges in order to maintain their control. But these changes would still result in a heightening of popular consciousness. The situation would be analogous to a prison in which an attempt is made to satisfy discontent by allowing prisoners to exercise outdoors. The result for the prisoners would be a heightened awareness of their imprisonment. When a minor social reform is made, people may gain an understanding of critical social problems and may push for even greater changes.

In describing the transition of consciousness Freire is trying to describe the developing political conditions in both the Third World and industrialized countries. He argues that the contradictions at the stage of naive-transitiveness foster the growth of a populist leadership which attempts to exploit the awakening consciousness of the people for its own gain. At this stage, because the masses cannot speak for themselves, they depend on populist leaders. At the same time intellectuals and students start to become engaged in social projects. Art becomes directed toward problems of concrete social reality. The inherent contradiction at this stage results from populist leaders allowing the participation of youth groups and intellectuals in the political process in order to control them. This allows for the development of revolutionary leaders within the political process itself. Freire's description of this stage of transition of consciousness sounds very much like the situation in the United States in the 1960's and early 1970's. Populist political leaders attempted to manipulate popular opinion by seeking help from intellectuals and youth and by using protests of these groups to cement their own political ranks.

For Freire, the revolutionary leadership would be comprised of those who help the masses move from the levels of semi-intransitive or naive-transitive consciousness to the level of critical consciousness. He argues that if the masses are not made the *subject* of the revolutionary process rather than its *object*, the revolutionary project will move to the right. A truly liberating revolution is one in which the people assume the role of active subjects in the transforming and recreating of the world. Freire sums up the difference between cultural action of the left and of the right: "The former problematizes, the latter slogan- izes." The right-wing revolutionary assumes that people have to be shaped to fit the "utopian" vision of the leaders. The left-wing revolutionary assumes that the people themselves must make the utopian vision.

For Freire the role of a critical consciousness cannot stop even with the birth of a revolutionary society. Critical consciousness plays a role in ejecting those cultural myths which remain. It is also "a force countering the bureau- cracy, which threatens to deaden the revolutionary vision and dominate the people in the very name of their freedom." While Freire does not speak directly of the Russian revolution, it is probably the example he had in mind. The failure of the revolutionary cause and the swing to the right in the Soviet Union can be linked to the defeat of the power of the local soviets and the end of the mass participation of the people in the revolutionary en- deavor.[21] The large-scale bureaucratic machinery that developed made the people into mere objects of economic and social planning, instead of active, critical subjects with control over social institutions. The new "socialist man and woman" have yet to be born in the Soviet Union.

Revolutionary change would not necessarily result from the contradictions arising under populist leadership, how- ever. The other possible direction, Freire believes, along with Illich and others, would be the creation of a mass society. This would involve a change in consciousness from the transitive state to a pathological form of "irrational consciousness." Highly technological societies may be moving toward a future where specialization in work becomes so narrow that people are generally incapable of thinking. In a dehumanized mass society, people no longer participate in the transformation of society. Freire writes, "Men begin thinking and acting according to the prescrip- tions they receive daily from the communications media rather than in response to their dialectical relationships with the world." In a mass society almost all consciousness of self is lost. Gone is the element of risk and planning on an individual level. "They do not have to think about even the smallest things; there is always some manual which says what to do in situation 'a' or 'b'." The mass society is a well-schooled society where people have given up independent thinking for mere learning based on expert advice. As in one of Freire's examples, "Rarely do men have to pause at a street corner to think which direction to follow. There's always an arrow which de-problematizes the situation." While street signs are not evil "they are among thousands of directional signals in a technological society which, introjected by men, hinder their capacity for critical thinking."[22]

While Freire's educational work grew out of a concern for the problems of South American society it has universal relevance as a definition of humanism and as an educational method. Obviously the method is not limited to one age group but can be applied to all people in all societies. If one applies the model to a country like the United States, for example, it raises some very important issues. It has already been suggested that within this framework minority groups in the United States can be considered as being at the level of a culture of silence·or at a level of intransitive consciousness. Furthermore, the majority of other Americans can be classified as being in a state of transitive consciousness or existing with the "irrational consciousness" of a mass society. The concept of mass society represents an extension of Freire's criticism of the banking method of education. The individual, an object within the mass society, is taught how to use his or her tools and conveniences properly. In such a society no situation becomes problematical or calls for individual praxis. People are dehumanized because of the lack of interrelationship between consciousness and practice.

It seems obvious what Freire's method means for a

country like the United States. It means that learning must result from praxis. Learning must be directly connected to social problems and used to solve those problems. It means a recognition of the teaching of reading as the most political act in the educational process. Language is the tool an individual uses to relate to his or her world. Taught in the manner of the banking method, it becomes a tool for the stifling of consciousness. Taught as part of a continued expansion of consciousness, it becomes an instrument for self-liberation. To be taught how to read in a situation which is completely abstracted from self-understanding is to be, in Illich's terms, "well-schooled." Black people in the United States certainly discovered this when they began to look closely at the white, small-town bias of public school text books.

One can go about implementing Freire's methods in various ways, depending on the skills and the imagination of the group leader. For instance, one might teach reading in a middle-class suburb by beginning with some thematic representation of a community problem—pollution, perhaps, or, on a more unsophisticated level for small children, one might take up such everyday themes as play, fights, or family problems. The leader and the children engage in a dialogue about the nature of the problem. From this initial dialogue words are taken that begin to form the basic text for reading. The children then work to solve the problem, reflect on their attempted solutions, add new words and stories to their readers and attempt to develop theories about the situation. In a poor urban area themes dealing with crime, poverty, family problems, and pollution could be used. In both examples the actual themes would not be chosen until after careful investigation. In this manner action, learning and consciousness would develop together.

FREIRE'S METHOD DEPENDS on dealing with real and important problems. The problems cannot be artificial classroom contrivances. This, of course, means that whether the method is trivialized or not depends on the group leader. Freire assumes that the contradictions of the culture of transitive consciousness will produce that revolutionary leadership. This optimism might not be shared by everyone.

There is also an assumption in Freire's method that people will *want* to become self-aware and that once this is accomplished, they will act in their own interests and in a *rational* manner. For what if people resist real freedom and self-awareness? The problem of individual freedom extends beyond just consciousness to include human character structure. For example, Wilhelm Reich argued that Marx would not have been able to explain the rise of fascism in Germany in the 1930's because he lacked the tools for understanding character structure, especially the particular character structure which sought the security of an authoritarian state. From this particular view the implementation of Freire's humanized world requires another element. It requires liberating the character structure of the individual so that self-awareness and a desire for self-determination become possible. It also implies that the establishment of a liberated world means changing child-rearing patterns and the family, so that people desire to be and can be free.

Betty Rothenberg

4

SEXUAL LIBERATION AND SUMMERHILL: REICH AND NEILL

CERTAINLY MAX STIRNER'S formulation of ownership of self and Paulo Freire's educational methods are meant to lead to basic changes in the individual. But one of the possible limitations of their arguments is that character structure is deeply rooted in the early stages of the child's psychic development. That is, whether a child develops an authoritarian or non-authoritarian style of social conduct might depend more on early development than on later forms of socialization such as formal education.

Concern about child-rearing practices and their relationship to political and social revolution has centered around the organization of the family itself. The value of collective child-rearing practices versus the traditional nuclear family is one of the major issues raised. The two most important figures in this dialogue have been Wilhelm Reich and A.S. Neill, who were closely associated in their work during their later years.

Wilhelm Reich's belief that the nature of child rearing was directly related to forms of social organization, resulted from his attempt to combine the sociology of Marx with a reinterpretation of Freudian analysis. Reich believed that it was possible for people to dispense with the irrationalism of politics and government and to establish what he called a "work-democracy" on the basis of a self-regulating character structure. This would be a society free of all authoritarian institutions—including the political state—where social relationships would evolve from *economic* organizations which would be created by the workers themselves. He linked the authoritarian character structure, which desired control by authoritarian institutions, to child-rearing methods and sexual repression. For Reich the central educational task of the twentieth century was sexual liberation and abolition of the patriarchal family. When in 1937 A.S. Neill, the founder of the Summerhill School in England, first met Reich, Neill said, "Reich, you are the man I've been looking for for years, the man who joins up the somatic with the psychological. Can I come to you as a student?"[1] This association with Reich, which began after their initial meeting in 1937, proved important in the development of Neill's ideas, as we shall see later.

TO UNDERSTAND REICH'S THEORY of the self-regulating character structure one must understand his differences with Freud. One of the basic points on which they differed was the nature of aggression. Freud, supporting an extremely conservative social philosophy, argued that aggression was an innate human instinct and that one's relationship to civilization and to oneself was best described in terms of conflict between the competing instincts of thanatos (death) and eros (love) and reality. In *Civilization and Its Discontents*, Freud claimed that social order could only be maintained by the repression and control of the aggressive death instinct. This control was the function of authoritarian institutions. Freud's picture of civilization is not pleasant or hopeful. Humanity is torn between eros, the passions of embracing the world, and thanatos, the desire to destroy it. As civilization progresses, the aggressive instincts have to be repressed, resulting in aggression toward self and increased feelings of guilt. For Freud the inevitable price humanity pays for the progress of civilization is increased authority and guilt.[2]

If accepted, these cultural pronouncements undercut the basis of utopian and revolutionary thought. Following Freud, the most that one could achieve would be an unhappy truce between one's self and society. And authoritarian institutions are necessary to control aggression and to guide the development of a strong superego. Freud's agrument is essentially one for "law and order." It suggests that if all police, laws, and traditional authoritarian child-rearing methods were dispensed with the result would be the unleashing of thanatos and a bloodbath of mutual destruction.

Reich rejected Freud's concept of a death instinct. Instead, he believed that cruel and aggressive character traits were the result of authoritarian, sexually repressive child-rearing practices. Sexual repression resulted in sexual anxiety, which in turn caused a general pleasure anxiety. Inability to experience pleasure and aggressive character traits, Reich argued, were always found together. On the other hand, ability to experience pleasure and non-hostile character traits were also linked. At the center of Reich's concept of pleasure were the sexual drives. Unlike Freud, who believed these drives were in *conflict* with the aggressive instincts, Reich saw aggressiveness as the product of the *repression* of sexual drives. In the 1920's, comparing sadistic and non-sadistic character traits, Reich wrote, "The mildness and kindness of individuals capable of genital satisfaction was striking in contrast. I have never seen individuals capable of genital satisfaction who had sadistic character traits."[3]

The revolutionary nature of Reich's argument was that it offered the possibility of planning a system of education and even organizing a whole society, so as to eliminate hostility and authoritarianism. It also suggested a method of analyzing political structures in terms of their child-rearing practices. Authoritarian and repressive political structures could be linked to educational practices which reflected the same traits. This, Reich argued in the *Mass Psychology of Fascism*, was certainly the case with the rise of fascism in Germany. He explained in *The Sexual Revolution* that because of the Russian revolution's failure to carry out the promises of its early years—the revolutionary moral codes and experimental practices in education and child rearing—it had resulted not, as he had hoped, in a non-repressive society, but in the emergence of an authoritarian one.

One of the primary aims of a revolutionary movement must be the freeing of the character structure of the people. This, Reich argued, could not be accomplished on a mass scale through the use of psychotherapy. While mental health clinics might be able to help a few patients, their overall impact was quite limited. In the 1920's, after eight years of work in a psychoanalytic clinic, Reich realized that "Psychoanalysis is not a therapy for large-scale application."[4] Patients in the clinic required a daily hour of therapy for at least six months. The only hope was in prevention. This meant ridding society of what Reich considered its most repressive institutions: compulsive marriage and the patriarchal family. Compulsive marriage refers to the traditional social demands that sexual relationships be limited to marriage and that marriage should be honored and maintained for the entire life of the partners. At the heart of these two institutions lay a repressive sexual morality.

84

Reich's emphasis on revolutionary institutional changes reflected his rejection of the conservative tendency of psychology and his interest in Marxist social philosophy. A distinction had to be made between reactionary psychology and social psychology. His example of this distinction involved the type of questions that might be raised about individuals who steal when they are hungry or go on strike when they are exploited. Reactionary psychology, Reich argued, would try "to explain the theft and the strike in terms of supposed irrational motives; reactionary rationalizations are invariably the result." On the other hand, social psychology would not feel it necessary to explain why some people steal when hungry or strike when exploited but would try to explain "why the majority of those who are hungry don't steal and why the majority of those exploited don't strike."[5]

The questions raised by social psychology, Reich felt, provided the missing ingredient in Marxist social philosophy. The scientific sociology of Marx did not have the tools to explain why all exploited workers did not strike. The rationale and techniques of exploitation could be explained by Marxism, but the workers' acceptance of exploitation could not be. Social-economic reasoning could not explain thoughts and actions which were *inconsistent* with economic interests and situations. Reich believed that Marx would not have been able to explain why a majority of German workers supported the rise of fascism. What was lacking in the freedom movements in Germany, Reich argued, "was a comprehension of irrational, seemingly purposeless actions or, to put it another way, of the cleavage between economy and ideology." What had to be realized was that it was not only the case, as Marx stated, that "the ideas of the ruling class are the ruling ideas" but that, as Reich stated, "every social order produces in the masses of its members that structure which it needs to achieve its main aims." In the case of fascism in Germany the supporting authoritarian character structure of the masses was a product of the repressive nature of the German family.[6]

Reich's goal was the elimination of cruelty and hostility in people's characters by bringing about major institutional changes. Reich held that the individual had a character armor which resulted in an inability to function spontaneously and naturally. This "armor" was a product of the historical experience of the individual. "The whole experiential world of the past was alive in the present in the form of character attitudes. The make-up of a person is the functional sum total of all his past experiences." Individual therapy was an attempt to break through these armored layers of character. Reich found that this therapeutic process revealed that the destructiveness in a person's character was nothing but anger "about frustration in general and denial of sexual gratification in particular." Destructiveness in the individual character was in this case a reaction to the inability to find pleasure. This inability to find or experience pleasure resulted in *pleasure anxiety* and *character armor* which both protected the individual from pleasure and produced hostility to all pleasure-producing experiences. Reich argued that pleasure anxiety and character armor could explain why people were willing to sacrifice their happiness to authoritarian institutions and social customs. Character armor not only drives people to a joyless life, but also makes them demand that *others* conform to authoritarian structures. The central mechanism of pleasure was, of course, sexual. Reich argued that as individuals encountered barriers to the satisfaction of the sexual urge, they began to hate. If there were no social outlets for expressing hatred, it became inhibited and internalized.[7] The type of character produced by this armoring was one most amenable to authoritarian or fascist political organizations.

It was primarily sexual anxiety, and pleasure anxiety in general, then, which inhibited the expression of both love and hatred. The individual not only developed destructive character traits, but was driven by anxiety to depend on authority. In the 1920's Reich realized, in what he himself later regarded as one of his most important conclusions, that "the orgastically unsatisfied individual develops an insincere character and a fear of any behavior which he has not thought out beforehand. . . ."[8] In other words, the individual becomes incapable of spontaneous and natural actions and seeks refuge in safe and dependent actions. Because of pleasure anxiety about acting, people are driven to seek security in an authoritarian structure which will dictate their actions.

Reich's utopian vision called for replacing this rigid character structure with a *self-regulating* character, thereby decreasing individual dependence on authoritarian structures. He noted that a breakdown in people's character armor brought about major changes in their social customs, work and independence. Individuals who had been highly moral suddenly found moralistic attitudes alien and queer. Reich wrote, ". . . they might have previously defended the principle of premarital chastity, now they felt such a demand as grotesque." Similar reactions took place with regard to work style. Individuals who had worked mechanically and viewed work as a necessary evil began to seek jobs in which they were interested. People whose jobs were already inherently interesting became more absorbed in their work. Teachers who had not been critical of present educational techniques began to find the usual method of treating children intolerable. The creation of a self-regulating character often led to a complete breakdown of the work ethic. Workers who had previously worked out of a compulsive sense of duty found the work unbearable once they were relieved of this compulsion.[9]

In many ways Reich's concept of self-regulated character is like Max Stirner's concept of ownership of self. For example, in contrasting moral regulation with self-regulation Reich wrote that, "the individual with a moral character structure performs his work without inward participation, as a result of the demands of a 'Thou shalt' which is alien to the ego."[10] Moral regulation created an armor which was not within the control of the individual. In Stirner's terms, it created moral duties which owned the individual. Or, as Reich wrote,

> The moralistic bureaucrat remains so even in bed. The healthy character type, on the other hand, is able to close up in one place and open up in another. He is in command of his armor, because it does not have to keep back forbidden impulses.[11]

For Reich a person with a self-regulated character was free of all hostility and conducted his or her life on the basis of desire and pleasure. Established moral codes were replaced with *individual regulation*. Reich, unlike Freud, did not believe this would lead to chaos. On the contrary, he saw people as being social and loving by nature. For example, women who were trapped in compulsive marriage and only performed the sexual act out of marital duty, lived a life of constant frustration. But free of compulsive marriage and pleasure anxiety, Reich argued, men and women would usually seek one mate who loved and satisfied them. This new kind of morality was to be governed by genital satisfaction and desire. "An unsatisfactory act was abstained from not because of fear, but because it failed to provide sexual happiness."[12]

It is important to realize that for Reich one of the most important elements in the sexual act was making the partner happy; this was one of the foundations of a satisfactory sexual experience. It was also the foundation of a non-repressive, non-authoritarian society. Self-regulation implied the ability to seek pleasure by trying to give someone else pleasure. The self-regulated character was one who was free of hostility, who owned himself or herself, who quested for pleasure and whose quest for pleasure meant giving happiness to others.

For Reich the heart of the sexuality problem was the compulsory monogamous marriage. In a study of anthropological literature written in 1931, Reich argued that the historical development of the patriarchial family and monogamous marriage paralleled the transition from a primeval economic work-democracy to the capitalist state. The concentration of wealth within one stratum of society resulted from the economic institution of marriage: in order to keep wealth within the family from generation to generation, the sexual activity of the female had to be restricted before and after marriage. Reich quoted from Engels' *The Origin of the Family*, "The first class-conflict that appears in history coincides with the development of the antagonism between man and woman in monogamous marriage and the first class-suppression with that of the female sex by the male sex. . . ."[13]

The economic function of the family gave way to an ideological function with the rise of the national state and industrialism. The family became the primary educational institution for training the child for an authoritarian society. Reich referred to the modern family as a "factory for authoritarian ideologies and conservative structures."[14] It was both the structure of the family and its repression of sexuality that prepared the child for the state. In the middle-class home, Reich argued, the father functioned within the family as the representative of the authority of the state.

The educational function of the family, too, was directly aimed at its own perpetuation. Children were sexually inhibited in preparation for future marriage. During the crucial ages of four to six they were usually denied the opportunity for sexual play and their attempts at masturbation were frustrated and condemned by their parents. Reich recognized certain class differences with regard to the treatment of children. In general, middle-class children were more inhibited than working-class children. This did not mean that working-class families were sexual paradises. On the contrary, many problems arose because of crowded housing and because of identification with the middle class.

An added problem for children within the family structure was that they became targets for the hostility and cruelty which resulted from their parents' own sexual repression. For parents, and especially mothers, children became the only content of their lives—to the great disadvantage of the children. Children came to "play the role of household pets whom one can love but also torture. . . ."[15] Children within the family structure were often objects of sadistic love, leading to the development of even more hostility within their own characters. With the family playing a major role in the education of the child, this relationship of hostility came to be perpetuated from one generation to another.

This combination of sadistic love, authoritarian structure, and sexual repression made the family the most important institution for political education. On the one hand, its function was to reproduce itself by "crippling people sexually." On the other hand, "[The family] creates the individual who is forever afraid of life and of authority and thus creates again and again the possibility that masses of people can be governed by a handful of powerful individuals."[16] It was not accidental, Reich contended, that conservative and reactionary youths were strongly attached to their families while revolutionary youth tended to reject their families.

It was in the *Mass Psychology of Fascism*, published in 1933, that Reich made his most brilliant statement of the relationship between compulsory sexual morality, the family, and the authoritarian state. The central question in his study of fascism was why people supported a party whose leadership was opposed to the interests of the working masses. In approaching this problem he made important distinctions between elements in each social class which supported Hitler's authoritarian dictatorship.

Small farmers, bureaucrats and the middle class, while different in terms of economic situation, shared the same family situation—the very situation which, as Reich had previously argued, produced the authoritarian personality. This family situation also promoted nationalism and militarism. The emotional core of ideas like homeland and nation, he argued, were the ideas of mother and family. The working class, however, had at one time displayed a somewhat looser family arrangement and thus had not been oriented so much toward nationalism as toward an international workers' movement. In the middle class, on the other hand, the family indeed was a nation in miniature and the mother was the homeland of the child. Reich quoted the Nazi Goebbels: "Never forget that your country is the mother of your life." On Mother's Day the Nazi press declared, "She—the German mother—is the sole bearer of the idea of the German nation. The idea of 'Mother' is inseparable from the idea of being German." As for militarism, Reich argued that it represented a substitute gratification for sexuality:

> The sexual effect of a uniform, the erotically provocative effect of rhythmically executed goose-stepping, the exhibitionistic nature of militaristic procedures, have been more practically comprehended by a salesgirl or an average secretary than by our most erudite politicians.

The forces of political reaction recognized this appeal, designing flashy uniforms and displaying recruiting posters which emphasized "foreign adventure" with the underlying implication of sexual freedom.[17]

Working-class support of fascism, Reich believed, owed its origin to working-class identification with the character structure of the middle class. During the tremendous period of physical and economic exploitation of the nineteenth century, the proletariat maintained a character structure rooted in the working class. In that period workers tended to identify with their own class; they were conscious of themselves as workers. But by the twentieth century, workers had alleviated their material condition— they had won shorter working hours, social security, and improved income. But rather than solidifying the workers' movement, this led to worker identification with the middle class. It was the purchase of the

> lower middle class bedroom suite, the learning of proper dance steps, the purchase of a "decent" suit of clothes and the attempt to appear respectable by suppressing sexuality that turned the revolutionary and communist into the reactionary.

All of these banalities of life, Reich argued, had a "greater reactionary influence when repeated day after day than thousands of revolutionary rallies and leaflets can ever hope to counterbalance." When the Depression destroyed the middle-class world, the working class, which had depended upon the middle class, turned to fascism. As Reich stated, "In times of prosperity this adaptation to middle-class habits was intensified, but the subsequent effect of this adaptation, in time of economic crisis, was to obstruct the full unfolding of revolutionary senti- ments."[18]

Reich's analysis of working-class support of fascism corresponds very closely to Freire's warning of how the oppressed identify with the oppressor; of how the internalization of an alien consciousness comes to dom- inate the people in the subordinate classes. For Reich working-class identification with the middle class resulted in a culture that was more stalwartly middle class than the middle class itself. In a search for "respectability" the working-class family became highly oppressive and authori- tarian. In a sense this happens to every apparently upwardly mobile group. For example, one could argue that the blue-collar worker in the United States has followed this path in an attempt to display middle-class respectability. It is certainly possible that black people in the United States, in an attempt to gain access to the dominant culture, will adopt the oppressive qualities of white middle-class respectability, impose harsh moral codes on their children, and attempt to do everything "correctly."

Reich believed that the Nazi Party was well aware that its support was grounded in the family and sexual repression. Mass individuals came to depend upon the Führer in the same manner as they had depended upon their fathers. The German fascist gave strong support to the idea of the family as the backbone of the nation and attempted to assure that the sexual act was associated only with reproduction in the national interest and not with pleasurable gratification. Reich quoted Adolf Hitler's 1932 presidential election statement that a woman's ultimate aim should be the creation of a family: "It is the smallest but most valuable unit in the complete structure of the state," Hitler stated. "Work honors both man and woman. But the child exalts the woman."[19]

In 1928 Wilhelm Reich founded the Socialist Society for Sexual Advice and Study in Vienna as an attempt to begin a major sexual revolution. Writing about this venture later in his life, he reflected upon the revolutionary implications of sexual freedom. Important social and economic changes would have to be made to solve the problems of adequate housing for adolescent sexual activity and for economic independence from the family. The sexual revolution also implies

> criticism of all political tendencies which based their existence and activity on man's essential helplessness; basic inner self-sufficiency of the human being; . . . self-guidance in children's education and in this way the gradual attainment of self-sufficiency for grown-ups.[20]

In 1930 Reich left Vienna and went to Germany because of what he felt were negative pressures placed on his social hygiene work. In Germany the Communist Party agreed to organize an association on the basis of Reich's ideas. This organization, the German Association for Proletarian Sexual Politics, issued a platform which contained the basic elements of Reich's plan. The program called for better housing conditions, the abolition of laws against homosexuality and abortion, the changing of divorce and marriage laws, the issuance of free contraceptives and birth-control advice, health protection of mothers and children, abolition of laws prohibiting sex education, and home leave for prisoners. Reich traveled throughout Germany giving lectures and establishing sex hygiene centers. Under pressure from the Nazis, Reich was forced to flee Germany for Copenhagen in 1933.

The year he left Vienna for Germany, Reich published his first major statement on sexual education, *The Sexual Revolution*. This book was written in reaction to what Reich labeled conservative sexual education and to what he perceived as the failure of the Russian revolution. Conservative sexual education, Reich believed, was attempting to remove the mystery from sexual relationships, and at the same time maintain traditional moral ideas. Venereal disease was stressed in most sex education courses in order to inhibit free sexual activity. Children were told about the beauty of the human body and the sexual act, but were advised to reserve sexual activity for the confines of marriage. For Reich there could be no such compromise between sexual education and established morality. It had to be a vehicle for sexual freedom and self-regulation.

Reich traced the development of sex and marriage laws in the Soviet Union from the radical policies of the early revolutionary period to the authoritarian policies of the late 1920's and 1930's, which he termed "Red Fascism."

This regression involved the attempt to re-establish the family as the center of education and authority. "In our fight for self-government of the children and for the elimination of the authoritarian form of the schools, we can no longer point to the S.U. [Soviet Union]." He argued that the rise of a totalitarian state, the end of sexual liberation, the re-establishment of the family as the center of the state, and the end of experimental and free education were all part of the same phenomenon.[2] [1]

Reich noted that as early as December 1917, Lenin had decreed that the husband was to lose his power of domination over the family and that women were to be given economic and sexual freedom and the right to determine their own names, residences, and citizenship. Marriage was made a purely secular occasion—the power of the church was removed. The family structure was further weakened by the institution of liberal divorce laws so that marriages could be dissolved by mutual consent. The education of children was to become a collective enterprise.

One of the schools that impressed Reich most during a visit to the Soviet Union in the late 1920's was Vera Schmidt's psychoanalytical home for children in Moscow. The school, founded in 1921, was what Reich referred to as "the first attempt in the history of education to give the theory of infantile sexuality a practical content." This school emphasized the development of self-regulation within the context of a community of children. Social adjustment would not be a product of moralistic judgment—which could not be understood by the child and only served the interests of the adult—but of the real social life of the children. Teachers at Vera Schmidt's school withheld all praise, blame, and judgments about the children's behavior. No violent displays of affection, such as embracing and kissing the child, were allowed, for they were only a means for adults to live out their own unsatisfied sexuality. Without disciplinary measures and moralistic judgment there would be no need for "patching up with kisses the harm one has done with beatings."[22]

Reich heartily approved of letting children work out their own social adjustment within a community of their peers. This removed them from the power of the family, which taught the child to follow authoritarian father and mother figures. Within the community of children the individual learned instead to act on the basis of self-need and self-regulation. Reich found support for these ideas in his study of anthropology. Among the Trobriand Islanders, who were one of Reich's fondest examples of a non-repressive sexual culture, children were given a great deal of freedom and independence from parental authority. Although parents would scold or coax their children, they would never issue a command to them nor speak to them other than as equals. One of the important results of this freedom was the ability of the children to form their own independent community. Children of Trobriand Islanders either remained with their parents during the day or joined their friends in a miniature republic. This community within the community functioned according to its own needs and desires. It provided both a vehicle for socialization which was free from authority, and a means of collective opposition to the parents.[23]

The most important element of self-regulation among the Trobriand Islanders and the children at Vera Schmidt's school was sexual self-regulation. At the psychoanalytical home no moral judgments were made with regard to sexual activities and children were taught to treat them like any other bodily function. Children were absolutely free to satisfy their sexual curiosity among themselves, mutually inspecting each other and viewing each other's naked bodies. This self-regulation of the sexual drives avoided the sexual anxiety and general pleasure anxiety which led to the development of an armored and authoritarian individual who could neither give nor receive pleasure.[24]

Freedom and community of the type found in the psychoanalytical home was essential for any meaningful, positive social change. Reich wrote, "The history of the formation of ideologies shows that every social system, consciously or unconsciously, makes use of the influencing of children in order to anchor itself in the human structure."[25] The method of sexual education, for instance, was directly related to the functioning of the economic enterprise. Self-regulated sexuality led to voluntary, free-flowing productive work; instinctual suppression led to work done as duty. It was in the context of this discussion of sexual and social self-regulation that Reich raised the traditional radical dilemma of whether the child should be indoctrinated into revolutionary beliefs.

The question was formulated in terms of how a self-governing and non-authoritarian society reproduced itself in its children. There were two possible methods of dealing with the problem. One was to indoctrinate with "revolutionary instead of patriarchal ideals." The other method was to give up the idea of revolutionary indoctrination and concentrate upon forming "the structure of the child in such a manner that it reacts of itself collectively and accepts the general revolutionary atmosphere without rebellion."[26] Reich, of course, argued for the latter because the real meaning of an ideology is determined by the character structure of the individual. A radical social philosophy could end in totalitarianism if preached and practiced by authoritarian personalities. The most important step for a self-governing society was to assure that it was free of authoritarian character traits.

In the last chapter of *The Sexual Revolution* Reich outlined the steps that should be taken to provide social and legal protection for infantile and adolescent sexuality. He called for the establishment of model institutions of collective education which would be the nuclei of the new social order. These institutions would function in a manner similar to Vera Schmidt's school, with scientific research being conducted to modify and improve techniques. Reich called for the distribution of birth-control devices on a mass scale. He also argued that, "A repetition of the catastrophic failure of the Soviet sexual revolution is unavoidable unless the room problem for adolescents and unmarried people is solved." This, Reich argued, could be accomplished by the government establishing emergency homes for youth. The population would have to be convinced that the government was uncompromisingly committed to ensuring the sexual happiness of all people. In addition to these changes Reich called for an extensive network of sexological institutions which would bring sexual instruction and enlightened discussions to the masses of the people. Children and adolescents should be protected against the implanting of sexual anxiety and sexual guilt feelings.

The ideal society of self-regulated character structures was called a work-democracy by Reich. In this society people would rid themselves of dependency upon political structures; rather, the formation of social organizations would flow directly out of necessary work activity. For Reich politics and political parties were irrational mechanisms for the enhancement of personal power and the promotion of dependency. The social irrationalism of politics was evidenced by the fact that society gave politicians great power to exercise judgments in areas where they were without competency. The power of the politician was analogous to that of the mystic. "A politician," he wrote, "is in a position to deceive millions of people, e.g., he can promise to establish freedom without actually having to do so. No one demands proof of his competence or of the feasibility of his promises." Politics in this sense functioned like religion and in fact represented a substitute for it. A mystic, like a politician, "can imbue masses of people with the belief that there is a life after death—and he need not offer the least trace of proof."[27]

In a self-regulated work-democracy the irrationalism of politics would be replaced with organizations growing out of the work situation. No government or political structure would be required to organize a system of railroads or conduct a postal system; these organizations would grow directly out of the social needs of transportation and mail delivery. People with self-regulated character structures would not submit to the authority of irrational politics and would demand social organizations which both served a need and provided a rational means of getting a particular task accomplished.

This dream, of course, was similar to the dream of traditional anarchism—the end of politics and the return of power to the people. Reich's important contribution to this debate was to highlight the importance of the relationship between personality and social structure. This brings us another step beyond Stirner's call for ownership of self and Freire's concern for an experiential awareness of social reality. In essence he was saying that an atmosphere of freedom helped to create a personality which demanded still more freedom. In the same manner, the ability to give love and pleasure depended upon the ability to experience love and pleasure. Repression of any sort decreased not only people's own pleasure but their ability to give love and make others happy. For Reich there could not be any compromise on this issue. If one wanted a society of self-regulated and non-sadistic individuals, one had to raise children in an atmosphere free from moral repression, authoritarian control, and pleasure anxiety.

IN THE LATE 1940's Reich wrote *The Murder of Christ*. Reich's description of Christ was his most poetic statement of the traits of a self-regulated, free, loving and spontaneous character. It was the "armored man (*sic*)" who killed

Christ and transformed his message into a religion of mysticism and repression. Christ spoke very plainly; his message gained mystery only because those armored individuals could not understand him. Christ must have recognized this fact when he quoted Isaiah:

> You shall indeed hear but never understand and you shall indeed see but never perceive. For this peoples' heart has grown dull, and their ears are heavy of hearing, and their eyes they have closed, lest they should perceive with their eyes, and hear with their ears, and understand with their heart, and turn for me to heal them.
>
> *(Matthew 13:14, 15)*

Reich wrote, "This is the ARMOR: No, they do not hear nor see nor feel with their hearts what they see and hear and perceive."

Christ was the symbol of the ability to love and give pleasure without robbing the world of joy. He was able to move with the currents of life and make his own life a pure statement of love. "The expression of Christ," Reich wrote, "has the quality of a meadow on an early sunlit spring morning. You can't see it, but you feel it all through you if you are not plague ridden." It was the armored individual, the "Red Fascist" and the person of "petit-bourgeois sentimentality," who could not feel that radiance. The world of work-democracy and genital freedom was to be populated with people who acted in the manner of Christ. Christ

> can laugh and scream with joy. He knows no restraint in his expression of love; in giving himself to fellow men, he does not lose a grain of natural dignity. When he walks on the ground, his feet set fully into the soil as if to take root with each step, separating again to take root again.[28]

A.S. NEILL HAD FORMULATED and practiced his ideas on education many years before his encounter with Reich in 1937. Over the years of friendship following their first meeting, Reich provided a psychological argument which pulled together many of Neill's ideas and influenced the self-regulative character of the education offered at Summerhill, Neill's school. Summerhill became the symbol for free school movements throughout the twentieth century—certainly it had a strong impact on the development of the free school movement in the United States in the 1960's. "Free school" eventually came to mean a school aimed at developing the self-regulative character structure in people.

Before meeting Reich, Neill claimed to have been influenced by a wide variety of people, including Adler, Freud, and Homer Lane. He admitted that he did not study psychology in any concentrated manner but just brought together those psychological arguments which made sense to him. His early philosophy was a blend of practical experience and popularized Freudian psychology. In the 1920's his dream was to spread the free school idea throughout the world; he even wrote Henry Ford to suggest that his factory might produce school caravans. In the 1930's Neill began to gain a critical understanding of the economics of capitalist society. It was this combination of Freud and radical political and economic analysis which made Summerhill an important institution of radical education in the twentieth century.

In establishing and operating Summerhill, Neill wanted to provide a means by which the world could be saved from crime, despair, and unhappiness. His early work must be understood in the context of the sense of failure and disillusionment that swept Europe after World War I. "Our education, politics and economics led to the Great War"; he wrote in the 1920's; "our medicine has not done away

101

with disease; our religion has not abolished usury and robbery. . . ." The source of the world's problems, and the major problem with the education of children, was the repression of natural drives. Neill plainly stated in *The Problem Child*, "I believe that it is moral instruction that makes the child bad. I find that when I smash the moral instruction a bad boy has received he automatically becomes a good boy."[29]

People, according to Neill, often found themselves in a state of conflict between the "life force" which is part of their nature, and the self which is created by moral instruction. Every action must be seen in terms of the tension between these two components. Moral instruction, then, tended to produce its opposite. A mother who suppressed a child's selfishness, for example, was ensuring that the child *would* be selfish. A person who stole was acting in a way which could be linked to repressive moral teaching in childhood. In Neill's identification of the existence of moral authority and conscience as the source of civilization's problems, he was following the tradition of anarchists like Max Stirner. In an imaginary dialogue with a "Mrs. Morality," he told this symbolic figure of authority that, "I believe there would be more honesty in the world if policemen were abolished. . . . It is the law that makes the crime."[30]

While at Reich's Institute in Maine during the late 1940's, Neill began to rewrite and condense his earlier works, claiming that, "I sat down to read them, and realized with something akin to horror, that they were out-of-date."[31] The weaving of these early ideas into Reichian thought did not prove difficult. The concept that morality produces hostility, aggression, and unhappiness received added support from Reich's concepts of character armor and pleasure anxiety. The one point, of course, upon which they immediately agreed was that a world free of hostility and aggression depended on total freedom for the child. Neill claimed Reich often chided him for not going far enough and encouraging adolescent sexual relations at Summerhill. "I told him," Neill wrote, "that to allow a full sex life to adolescents would mean the end of my school if and when the government heard about it."[32]

The one idea that Neill did not alter was the distinction between freedom and license in a free school. Freedom meant freedom from moral teachings, not the right to commit any action. In response to the question of what he would do if a boy were pounding nails into a grand piano, he said, "It doesn't matter if you take the child away from the piano so long as you don't give the child a conscience about hammering nails." In other words, he argued that one can stop a person from doing something without making it a form of moral punishment. Another example Neill gave was of a child leaving a tool out in the rain. In this case the rain was harmful to the object but not morally *good* or *bad* in an abstract sense. To provide freedom for the child meant to provide him or her with the opportunity of growing up without an internalized moral authority or conscience.[33]

Neill's concept of freedom was very close to Stirner's idea of ownership of self. Neill wrote, "To give a child freedom is not easy. It means that we refuse to teach him religion or politics or class-consciousness." Freedom was the right to own or choose one's own ideals and beliefs; the function of a free school was to provide the necessary institutionalization of this concept. Summerhill reflected Neill's statement of the 1920's, "No man is good enough to give another his own ideals."[34] It was to be a place where the individual could explore and make choices about those ideals.

By the 1930's Neill had begun to link his educational ideas with radical political thought. For instance, in 1935 a magazine presented Neill and two other headmasters in England with a series of questions dealing with obedience and authority in the educational process. They were asked to what extent they thought the free development of the individual clashed with the interests of the state, and whether the desire for freedom could be combined with a sense of responsibility. The two school officials replied in general liberal terms about the school promoting cooperation and a sense of responsibility toward the state. Neill answered with a statement that the state at that time represented a capitalist system which emphasized the instinct of possession over that of creation. Within a capitalist state, he argued, ". . . there is no hope of creative love as opposed to possessive love. Only under some form of Socialism have freedom and love and education a chance." For Neill the answer to the question depended on the nature of the state. If the state were capitalistic and authoritarian, then the free development of the individual would clash with its interests. On the other hand, "The free development of the individual will not clash with the interests of the State if the latter is just and humane and loving."[3][5]

In 1939 Neill wrote *The Problem Teacher*, a book which detailed the relationships he was beginning to see between the nature of schooling and political and economic systems. In it he stated bluntly that, "The State schools must produce a slave mentality because only a slave mentality can keep the system from being scrapped." He suggested that there was a direct link between Hitler's method of control and an educational system which produced humble yesmen. In general his argument followed the pattern of the traditional radical critique of schooling as a function of the interests of the state. In Germany and Italy national schooling meant fascism; in England it meant preparing each generation to fit into a capitalist economy. The English schools not only produced a slave mentality but also robbed the working class of effective leadership—a point which must be considered one of the most important criticisms of the development of the secondary school in both England and the United States. "The master stroke in . . . educational policy," he wrote, was the secondary school, the school that took children of the working class to white-collar jobs in clerking, teaching, doctoring and the other professions. Thus it robbed the workers of its best men and women. . . .[36]

Neill's critique of schooling was now beginning to reflect some of the influence of his recent contacts with Reich. The home, he argued, was the state in miniature, and it was because it provided this training in obedience that every state gave so much emphasis to the home. But Neill took Reich's argument one important step further. He insisted that the power of the school was based on its reproduction of family life. "Theoretically one would think that schooling is an antidote to family influence. It isn't: it is family life on promotion." Neill went on to draw parallels between the father as head of a family and the teacher as head of a family of forty or more children. In fact, the situation within the school might be worse than that in the family, because the teacher did not necessarily have the love most fathers felt for their children. Within the school the hostile side of the father was emphasized through the teacher. "And this is true of the disciplinarian," Neill wrote, "for he has no love to give out, only hate."[37]

This attack on the family and established schools did not imply abolition of those institutions, but their modification through the spread of Summerhill-type schools. Writing in 1944, he expressed hope that a socialist state could be established and with it, a national system of boarding schools. "Naturally," he wrote, "I want to specify that such a school will be a free school, with self-government and self-determination of the individual child, that is, I visualize a nation of Summerhills." The spread of such schools would not eliminate the family but provide a means for the child to escape the narrow confines of the nuclear family. The small family, Neill argued, was not good enough for the child. It was not only authoritarian but repressive in terms of its lack of a broad community of contacts. In schools like Summerhill, the child would not only be free of the authority of the family but would also be in the stimulating company of a wide variety of self-governing people. Neill sadly recognized that most people would not agree with his ideas: "Most people believe in discipline (for others); most think that a child should be treated like a fruit tree and pruned regularly."[38]

It should be emphasized that Neill, throughout the existence of Summerhill, firmly held that freedom alone was the only cure for most "problem children." But like Reich, Neill was concerned about how mass therapy could be conducted. By the 1940's he had come to the conclusion that analysis was not a necessary therapeutic technique. The mere *practice* of freedom was the therapeutic tool. Any person could help problem children provided that person understood and believed in freedom. Like Reich, Neill came to believe that radical therapy did not involve the treatment of individual patients but the removal of those social conditions which caused repression.

It was from this standpoint of radical therapy that Neill criticized the general trend of Freudianism. The failure of most Freudians, he argued, was their unwillingness to link themselves with some social movement. "Psycho-analysis has linked up with nothing. It knows that the father complex is evil, yet it does not begin a campaign to abolish fear and authority in the school."[39] Neill admitted that without Freud, Summerhill would not exist. But what Summerhill had accomplished, and where most of the psychoanalytic movement had failed, was in bridging the gap between theory and actual social organization. Summerhill was an attempt to establish an institution to rid society of the problems defined by Freudian theorists. In this sense, Summerhill represented radical social therapy.

IN 1947 NEILL MADE his first trip to the United States, where he stayed with Reich at his Institute in Maine. During his stay Neill wrote *The Problem Family*. In this book he argued that socialism was not sufficient to ensure the happiness and freedom of humanity. He echoed Reich's ideas when he wrote, "I want Socialism plus sex-economy, nationalization plus relaxed bodies, for if the body is relaxed the chances are that the psyche is pretty free."[40] Neill rejected his previous leanings toward established socialist and communist movements; he also rejected solutions based on politics and political democracies. What he accepted was a Reichian work-democracy where self-regulated individuals would reject the irrationalism of politics and form social organizations out of need and desire. The free life of Summerhill was now the prototype of the work-democracy.

In *The Problem Family* Neill reiterated his own idea—and Reich's—that the heart of civilization's problems was the organization of the family. Again he linked the organization of the family to that of the state and the school. Neill now defined schools as products of direct class interest, used

> to discipline the workers in such a way that they are symbolically castrated for life, the aim being to continue the privileges of the rich, who will be safe with an under class that has been unmanned and therefore has not the guts to rebel.[41]

The problem for modern society was to choose between the free and unfree family.

The free family was one in which children were freed from the internalized authority produced by moral discipline. This *could* be done within the family. "In families many parents do it," Neill wrote, "and there are quite a lot of children living today who will never spank a child or moralize about sex or give a fear of God."[42] Freedom within the family would then be reflected in the school and in society in general. Freedom within the family, for example, implied the abolition of compulsive marriage. Marriage would be held together only by the love of the two partners. The free family, Summerhill and work-democracy were all interrelated parts.

For both Reich and Neill education and upbringing were directed toward encouraging the growth of free, self-regulated individuals. They did not use the word "freedom" in the liberal sense of freedom before the law or political freedom, but in the Stirnerian sense of ownership of self. One was truly free of authority when one was free of guilt. Reich and Neill added a new dimension to libertarian education by grounding the problem of freedom in the actual psychic growth of the child.

I rane. Wolfson

5
FREEING THE CHILD FROM CHILDHOOD

WHILE WILHELM REICH and A.S. Neill considered liberation of the child from the moral confines of the nuclear family, they did not consider liberating the child from the very concept of childhood. In their solutions the process of child rearing would simply be transferred from the nuclear family to a community of children. This meant perpetuating a period of childhood and youth during which children would be kept in a state of dependency, isolated from the major social and economic forces of society. Neill in a sense was trapped by modern concepts of childhood and youth into assuming that abolition of control by the nuclear family required the substitution of *another* controlling institution. The solution he found in Summerhill left unanswered the questions of whether collective child-rearing practices might not be as harmful or more harmful than the nuclear family and whether the problem of the nuclear family might not be solved only by breaking through the confines of the modern concepts of childhood and youth. Perhaps any meaningful concept of freedom must include the actions and activities of children.

One way of approaching the problem of the relationship of the child and the family is to consider it in terms of historically changing concepts of childhood and adolescence. One of the important historical arguments that has been given for liberating the child from the nuclear family and the modern concept of childhood can be found in Philippe Ariès' modern classic, *Centuries of Childhood*. Tracing the interrelated development of the concepts of childhood, family, and the school, he argues that the concept of childhood is a very recent one in Western culture. During the Middle Ages, as soon as an infant left swaddling clothes she or he was integrated into the adult world and shared the same games, social life, and styles of clothing. Children were not segregated, nor were they defined as a special category. Similarly, the family at this time did not exist as a small nuclear unit. Marriage was not given much significance and was primarily an economic institution for passing on the family name and wealth. Of much greater importance was the *community*, which provided the major focus of social activity and was the major agency of socialization. It was this community, consisting of people of all ages, into which the child was integrated.

After the Middle Ages the concept of the child, the importance of the small nuclear family, and the role of the school all developed along parallel lines and reinforced each other. The school helped to mark off the special age periods of childhood development and taught the family that it must direct special attention to the well-being of the child. The child was withdrawn from the adult community and given a special status which included different expectations and a separate social life. The family began to define itself as a small, detached, nuclear unit.

Ariès concludes with,

> Our world is obsessed by the physical, moral and
> sexual problems of childhood. . . . Family and school
> together removed the child from adult society. . . .
> The solicitude of family, Church, moralists and
> administrator deprived the child of the freedom he
> had hitherto enjoyed among adults.

Prior to the modern family, an individual's social relationships were mainly within a broad community and this created a greater degree of sociability. Conversely, Ariès links the modern trend toward individualism with the development of the small modern family, going so far as to state: "One is tempted to conclude that sociability and the concept of the family were incompatible, and develop only at each other's expense."[1]

What Ariès' study suggests is that if we truly want to change this type of family structure, we must get rid of the concept of childhood and the idea that there should be institutions which attempt to make the child into some particular moral or social ideal. This would mean the elimination of the school. In its place we would see the development of the child as an *independent being* and his or her integration within the social structure.

Recent studies of the development of the concept of adolescence and youth culture have tended to support these interrelationships found between the family, school, and specifically defined age categories. These studies also take up an aspect of the problem that Ariès did not fully consider—one that has important implications for any future planning—the effect of industrial organization on changing concepts of childhood and youth. Concepts of childhood and youth, these studies show, can be directly related to the changing value of these age groups in the industrial process. In the nineteenth century children of the lower classes were an important element in the labor supply for factories in developing industrial countries like the United States and England. Children of the lower class were without childhood in the sense that at an early age they entered the industrial workplace. Middle-class children, on the other hand, were needed for a developing white-collar class. This required special training in schools, which meant they were withheld from the labor market and kept in a state of dependency upon the family.[2]

In the United States in the late nineteenth century a combination of factors resulted in the displacement of more and more children and adolescents from the labor market. There was a feeling by industrialists that technological changes no longer required the use of children in factories, a concern by labor unions that cheap child labor depressed the wage scale, and an increase in the need for white-collar workers. Beginning in the 1920's, increases in man-hour productivity were reflected in the displacement of more youth from the labor force and an increase in high school enrollments. Young people were simply not needed in an economic system increasingly dependent on machines.

One effect of these changes was the development of a concept of adolescence with its own psychology and cultural style. This was reflected in the development of something called the "youth problem." In the 1920's "the youth problem" was seen as part of the Jazz Age; in the 1930's it was called the Lost Generation; after World War II it took the form of the Beat movement; and in the 1960's it was related to the Hippies and Yippies.[3]

Another important consequence of these changes was the extension of the child's dependency on the family. While most people think of the school as threatening the nuclear family, in fact the opposite might be true. As children and youth were removed from the labor market and placed in school they became dependent on the family for a longer and longer period. By the middle of the century, in many families in the United States this dependency extended until college years. The structure of schooling required the maintenance of families as places from which children were sent to school. Rather than the school weakening the family structure by taking over some of its functions, the family was probably strengthened by the increased dependence of children and youth.

GIVEN THIS CONSIDERATION of the historical development of the concept of childhood and dependency on the nuclear family, the collective child-rearing practices of Summerhill appear in a somewhat different light. First, collective child-rearing practices certainly would weaken the family in that the major responsibility for child rearing would be transferred to a community like Summerhill. But this might not have any effect on family organization if the father and mother of the child were required to pay for their child's care until adolescence or later. The situation would be similar to any other middle-class family sending its children to boarding school. The family would still be required as a legal and economic institution until the child reached some socially defined stage of adulthood. The school would therefore only be truly effective in weakening the nuclear family if the mother and father were freed from legal and economic responsibility for the child while it was very young.

Second, collective child-rearing practices would have an important effect on the social role of women. Freed from extended periods of responsibility for child rearing, women would be able to enter the labor market on more equal terms with men. The liberation of women was an important concern to Reich and Neill, and is one of the major forces shaping the present development of collective child-rearing practices like day-care centers. But again, this only had meaning if the mother is freed from economic and legal responsibility for the child.

Third, collective child-rearing practices *do* free the child from the family but *not* from the state of dependency inherent in the very concept of childhood: in this case, dependency upon a community, school, or the state. This situation carries with it a certain amount of irony. According to Ariès, the development of the concept of childhood was a major force in the development of the modern family. Collective child rearing attacks the family without calling into question one of the important elements which caused its existence.

From this perspective collective child rearing might be of more benefit to the parents than to the child. One of Reich's and Neill's hopes, of course, was that if children were liberated from the moral structures of the family, they would develop non-authoritarian character structures. The important question is whether this would occur. If collective child rearing were placed under government control and directed toward the traditional aims of public schooling, it seems unlikely that it would. These doubts are confirmed by recent studies of the collective child-rearing methods of the Israeli Kibbutz. The Kibbutz represents an attempt to solve the problems of women's equality and the family through collective methods. It is a good illustration of the inner dynamics of the problem and it suggests that solutions based on collective child rearing might result in the creation of a non-rebellious and totally group-conformist type of personality.

The Kibbutz movement represents one of the most important twentieth-century experiments in developing a society that would provide equality for all its members. It has established agricultural communities with collective ownership of the tools of production and democratic control. Within the Kibbutz movement there has been an attempt to maintain economic and occupational equality. Collective child-rearing methods have been developed and the nuclear family has been de-emphasized, partly in order to establish equality for women and free them from the burden of child rearing.

116

The evolution of and interconnection between female equality, changing family patterns, and collective child-rearing practices in the Kibbutz received its earliest consideration in the United States in the work of anthropologist Melford E. Spiro in the early 1950's. In 1951 he lived on a Kibbutz which traced its origins to the early 1920's. It had been founded primarily by Jewish youth of Polish origin who, coming out of the youth movements in Europe, combined a pastoral romanticism with radical rejection of traditional Jewish customs. They emphasized a rejection of city life for the hard work of an agricultural community. They also sought to replace the traditional Jewish family with a form of cooperative living.[4]

When the Kibbutz was founded, one of the main concerns was the equality of women. The importance and compulsiveness of marriage were reduced and the sexual relationship was viewed as a personal affair, with neither the original union nor its termination requiring the sanction of the community. The marriage relationship was announced essentially by a couple asking for a joint room, and divorce by the couple asking for separate rooms. By the 1950's the Kibbutz had become part of the State of Israel and the law required that a child had to be born of married parents in order to receive civil rights; therefore, official marriage on this Kibbutz occurred with pregnancy.

Reducing the importance of marriage, it was believed, would reduce the social and economic dependency of the woman on the man. The abolition of the marriage ceremony was meant to remove women's legal subjection to men. The female did not assume the male's name nor was her legal status that of "his wife." Within this Kibbutz a female's prestige was not enhanced by the fact that her husband was a great worker or brilliant leader. Because of the collective ownership of property the female was not economically dependent on the male. The traditional sexual division of labor was destroyed. Men and women were to have similar occupational roles. Spiro found,

117

however, that the ideal of women's equality had been compromised by what was referred to as women's "biological tragedy."

Over the long years of development work had become divided on the basis of sex. This was due partly to the strenuous nature of some of the labor, but even more significantly to the fact that pregnant women could not work for long periods in the fields and nursing mothers had to work near the Infant House. This meant that when women were forced to leave vital agricultural pursuits, their positions were assumed by men. Consequently, on the Kibbutz where Spiro lived, 88 percent of the women were involved in service jobs, the largest numbers working in education and the laundry.[5]

Hand in hand with this reduction in the importance of marriage went a de-emphasis on the role of the family. Certain traditional types of family functions were collectivized. One important step was the establishment of a common dining room. People were not to separate into nuclear families at mealtime—an occasion which had traditionally performed a unifying function for the family. In fact, the traditional family meal represented all the values the members of the Kibbutz wanted to reject: the father sat as patriarchal leader of the family while the female displayed her subservient role by serving the food. In the collective dining room males and females shared the cooking and cleaning. The meal itself became a community affair rather than a family affair. In fact, the children ate in their own separate dining facilities.

The emphasis on the family was also reduced with the collective education of children. On this particular Kibbutz, collective education began four days after birth, when the baby and mother were released from the hospital. At this age the child entered the "Children's Society" in which it remained until graduation from high school and election into the Kibbutz. As the child grew up, it lived in a series of "houses." The Infant House handled a maximum of sixteen infants ranging in age from four days to approximately one year and was supervised by a nurse and three assistants drawn from the labor supply of the community. The infants were not allowed to be taken to their parents' rooms until they were six months old, so that most personal needs were attended to by the nurses. Infants were with their parents only during feeding time or during parental visits to the Infant House on weekday afternoons and Saturdays.

At the age of six months the children were allowed one hour a day away from the Infant House to visit their parents' rooms; at one year this was increased to two hours a day and the children were taken from the Infant House to the Toddlers House. There they were placed under the supervision of a new nurse, gradually toilet trained, and taught to feed themselves. They learned to play with children of the same age group. The size of the social group in the Toddlers House was about eight children. At the age of four or five years the children left this group and entered Kindergarten. The size of the community of children at this time was increased to sixteen. This established the social group the child would be with until the end of high school.

The children were therefore not raised in a family but in a community of peers. They lived in a dormitory, visited their parents for two hours a day, and shared all the rest of the day with their peers. There was little differentiation by sex in this process. Boys and girls shared the same showers, toilets, and rooms. They were accustomed to sharing activities and viewing each other's bodies. Sexual matters were discussed quite openly and were not hidden from the children. However, sexual activity itself was discouraged until the individual entered the Kibbutz.[6]

The importance of the Kibbutz education was that it consciously attempted to maintain female equality by eliminating the importance of the nuclear family in child rearing. It was hoped that female equality would be insured by a collective education which practiced sexual equality and which abolished the social role of mother.

The question that must be raised about this process has to do with the psychological effects of being raised in a community of peers. What does such a form of child rearing mean in terms of power and authority relationships within a society? The psychological effects of child rearing on the Kibbutz have been studied by a variety of experts.[7] Probably the most important writing on the relationship between child-rearing practices and social structure has been Bruno Bettelheim's *The Children of the Dream*.

One of the important consequences of collective child rearing, Bettelheim has argued, is the development of a collective superego or collective conscience—what Max Stirner had referred to as the "spook" of internalized authority. Bettelheim recognizes that this development within the Kibbutz had important implications for other Western cultures. Within the Kibbutz, the source of the superego is no longer the parents but the children's society. This is precisely the trend in other Western societies like the United States, where the role of the parent is decreasing and the importance of the peer group increasing. "If this trend continues," he writes, "the superego in our society, too, may come to be based more and more on a morality that derives from the need to cooperate with the peer group, as is already true in the kibbutz."[8]

For Bettelheim the superego which is the product of a peer group is less awesome, more familiar, and more inescapable. In the middle-class family the source of authority is the parents, with support from other authority figures like the police or God. In the Kibbutz the superego is a product of collective demands and is less often presented as a threat. On the Kibbutz the individual, as part of the peer group, participates directly in the forming of her or his own superego. Since the individual ego helps to form the superego, there is less of a tendency toward the separation of the two and the development of conflict. There is also less guilt and anxiety, because to meet the demands of the superego is to meet the demands of the community. In other societies morality, particularly sexual morality, makes demands that have no relationship to the real life of the community, creating conflict for the individual. With the collective superego, however, there is less conflict because the demands of the collective super-ego reflect the demands of the environment.

Bettelheim's argument suggests that the abolition of the nuclear family might have some very positive results in terms of the reduction of individual emotional conflict. On the other hand, it might result in even more powerful forms of control. Middle-class children can remove themselves from their parents, hold them at a distance. But Kibbutz children never escape the watchful eyes of their peers; moreover, the individual on the Kibbutz is made a *part* of the controlling system. "We can never hide from a control system for which we are quite consciously a part," writes Bettelheim. For the Kibbutz child "the commands are more inescapable because there is nowhere a dissenting voice to support one's own doubts or dissent."[9]

Being raised in a community of children also makes it difficult to separate one's own ego from that of the group. In the Kibbutz little time or emphasis can be given to private feelings and emotions; children can rarely be alone and outside the control of the group. According to Bettelheim, "Group sanctions are all the more effective because with no way to escape the group, there is no way to escape its rejection."[10] If one does try to run counter to the demands of the group, there are no supporting values for this revolt, no place to escape the values of the group. Growing up in a community of children provides very few opportunities to experience oneself as being separate from the group.

Children of the Kibbutz also exhibit an emotional flatness and an inability to express deep emotional feelings that Bettelheim links to the process of collective child rearing. In the first place, group education allows very little time or opportunity for the experiencing of private emotion or an emotion shared intimately by only one or two friends. Again, one finds no support for the private experience. Bettelheim suggests that in the Kibbutz,

> Emotion shared with only one other person is a sign of selfishness no less than other private possessions. Nowhere more than in the kibbutz did I realize the degree to which private property, in the deep layers of the mind, relates to private emotions.[11]

Second, group life often requires the repression of strong emotional feelings. This is particularly true during adolescence, when sexual relations on the Kibbutz are not sanctioned but at the same time adolescent girls and boys are sharing rooms, toilets, and showers. This condition promotes a high degree of sexual stimulation yet at the same time requires the repression of that drive. Third, Bettelheim suggests that the range and possibilities of emotional experience are limited in collective child rearing. The child feels a great deal more secure in the group than in a nuclear family. On the Kibbutz the group is the god on which the person depends. In the family it is the mother and the father. The Kibbutz child never feels the anxiety of possibly losing her or his source of security. Bettelheim argues that a middle-class child's dependency on the parents and fear of losing them results in a process of introjection whereby the child internalizes the parents as a means of possessing them. For Bettelheim, the process of introjection trains the child in the ability to assume the role of others and speculate about different ways of living. When asking Kibbutz youths questions like, "How do you think you would have felt about kibbutz life if you'd been born and raised in the city?" he would receive answers like, "I wasn't raised there, so I can't answer that." "To move outside the self and take a look at it," Bettelheim observes, "was not a stance common to these youngsters."[12]

Bettelheim's description of the effects of collective child rearing raises some very interesting questions. For instance, while the nuclear, triangular family can be viewed as a source of dependency on authoritarian figures, it can also be seen as providing an opportunity for the child to separate herself or himself from the rest of society and develop a private self. This separation of self through the mechanism of the family can be viewed in both a positive and negative light. Negatively it can be argued that the individualism spawned by the family leads to a selfish individualism which works against social cooperation. This is one of the arguments given in favor of the collective education of the Kibbutz in that it fosters social cooperation. On the positive side it can be argued that the family situation allows for the type of social separation and conditions basic to developing the mechanism of revolt. Revolt against the family is the first step in throwing off the control of society.

One can argue from this perspective that the major problem with collective child rearing and the development of a collective superego is that this superego is all-controlling and does not provide mechanisms for individual rejection or revolt. This may make little difference in the Kibbutz, where there is collective ownership and control. But in advanced industrial countries the spread of collective child-rearing practices would not necessarily imply a total reform of the social system. If previous experience is any guide, schools have always tended to reflect the inequalities of society.

The questions raised about the Kibbutz can be directed toward Summerhill as well. Certainly Neill envisioned a series of Summerhills as part of a socialist society. This would supposedly make collective child rearing a part of a just society. But it should be recognized that the dynamics of Western society which are currently providing impetus for collective child rearing are directed *not* toward the liberation of the child but toward the liberation of women from the trap of the home. Within this context, collective child rearing simply *institutionalizes* the existing patterns of society as far as children are concerned. It is a dreary prospect to think of public schools operating child-care centers. That would be the final triumph of the process of schooling.

This also raises the question of whether present trends in collective child rearing would only provide for women's escape from the burden of the home and not for female liberation. Feminists like Emma Goldman argued that there could be no women's liberation as long as society retained its present form of organization. Writing in the early twentieth century, she argued that it was certainly not any glorious independence for women to be forced to type in offices, to sew in sweat shops, or to stand behind counters in department stores. For Goldman work of this nature was ample reason for women to rush into marriage at the first offer to escape their supposed "independence." To liberate women would mean to liberate society from its existing social and economic structure.[13]

ONE SOLUTION TO THIS DILEMMA might be to reverse the problem and think of it in terms of freeing the child from the family, releasing the child from a state of dependence upon controlling institutions. The problem with the collective education of the Kibbutz is that it serves a particular end and does not allow for the self-development of the individual separate from the group. If the Kibbutz schools were eliminated and the children at an early age were integrated into the adult life of the community, that might provide a partial solution. The fact that formal schools exist on the Kibbutz appears as a cultural remnant of middle-class society. The founders of the Kibbutz assumed that schools were a natural part of all societies. But in the drive for women's rights, it should not be assumed that the best solutions lie in the expansion of schooling.

This argument leads back to the possible solution of simultaneously liberating children from the modern category of childhood *and* emancipating women from the burden of extended periods of child rearing. This solution suggests two possible directions we might take. The first possibility is to organize society so that all people, including children, have a useful social role. In the twentieth century the rise of schooling and the increase in early retirement are directly connected to higher productivity and advanced technology. Essentially our economy has told young people and older people that they are no longer useful. Youths are put into schools and older people are sent to retirement communities. To change this would mean viewing the child as a miniature adult, with all the rights and status of adulthood. As Ariès found to be the case during the Middle Ages, the child would participate in adult activities and would be treated as an adult.

The second possible direction would be to accept the separation of production and consumption that exists in our society for certain age groups—that is, to accept the fact that children and youth function as consumers but not as producers. Right now, of course, this situation only breeds greater dependence; in the proposed solution, however, children and youth up to a certain age, such as twenty-one, would be given a guaranteed income which would allow them to leave home at an early age without necessarily having to attend a custodial institution. The young people would be allowed to spend that income in any manner they chose. This would destroy children's dependency on the family and school, and would end the obligation of the woman to assume the responsibility for a lengthy period of child rearing. The proposal would have an advantage over the previous one in that it might avoid the exploitation of children and youth by the industrial process. It would have the disadvantage of possibly keeping children financially dependent on the state.

While the above proposals are only speculative, they do suggest possible goals. If the abolition of the nuclear family is an essential step in the drive toward women's emancipation, it would be better, and essential in the long run, for the child to be liberated in the process than to be subjected to an expanded system of control through schooling. This liberation requires that the barriers of modern concepts of childhood be transcended. At as early an age as possible the child must become a miniature adult, a person exercising all the rights and privileges that we now confer on adults.

CERTAIN LIBERTARIAN GOALS might be achieved if society broke through modern concepts of childhood. Such concepts treat the child as an object and not as a subject of the social process. Viewed as an object to be worked upon, the child becomes a focal point for the imposition of ideals and ideologies. In the United States in the twentieth century we have witnessed repeated attempts to solve social problems, ranging from poverty to venereal disease, by attempting to shape the character of the child in the school. Because the child has been viewed as an object, childhood has become a dumping ground for a myriad of attempted solutions of social problems. If children became subjects or participants in the shaping of society, they would become actors in the making of history. As Paulo Freire suggests, the difference between being human and being animal-like is the exercise of consciousness and the participation as a subject in the making of history. The child treated as an object is treated as an animal. The child treated as a subject would be treated as a human being.

Nadia Keyser

6
PRESENT REALITIES AND FUTURE PROSPECTS

THE THEORIES OF EDUCATION discussed in this book represent one aspect of the battle for control of the mind of the child that has occurred over the nineteenth and twentieth centuries. Any consideration of their value and meaning must be made against the background of the present organization and purposes of education and an evaluation of the present possibilities of social change through the use of educational techniques. Radical theories of education have been based on an assumption common to most modern societies—that one of the key elements in organizing a society is the nature of the educational and child-rearing system. It is this system which shapes the future members of society.

The real disagreements, therefore, go beyond educational technique; they involve the very nature of social change. Theories of education are just one very important aspect of an overall theoretical perspective about how society should change. We can identify fundamental differences in theoretical perspectives about social change in different educational methods. Two distinct models emerge. One model has a technological and rationalistic orientation which seeks social improvement through more orderly social planning and increased efficiency. This is a model which in the twentieth century has tended to cut across ideological lines; it has been embraced by liberal, fascist, and communist countries alike. This model is concerned primarily with increased economic productivity and social stability. Society is conceived of as a machine with the goal of efficient operation. People become "human resources" whose values are determined by their contribution to the smooth functioning of the social machinery.

In this model the child is treated as an object to be worked upon and shaped for the good of society. As I have demonstrated in another book, this is the model of the "good society" that pervaded the organization of the public schools in the United States in the twentieth century. The modern high school, vocational guidance, and testing were all conceived of as means of increasing the efficiency of the social machinery. The raw human resources of children would be classified, sorted, and shaped, then sent from the schools into their proper niches in society.[1]

The nature of the other model of social change may be deduced from the philosophies of education considered in this book. Here the concern is not with order and efficiency but with increasing individual autonomy. The goal of social change is increased individual participation and control of the social system. This model rests on the conviction that a great deal of the power of modern social institutions depends on the willingness of the people to accept the authority and legitimacy of these institutions. In this context the question becomes, not how to fit the individual into the social machine, but *why* people are willing to accept work without personal satisfaction and social authority which limits freedom. This condition of acceptance, as has been argued in this volume, is primarily the result of the ideals, beliefs, and ideologies in the mind of the child. As a result, the individual believes it is one's duty to work for some good which might not have any relationship to one's own needs and desires. The goal of this libertarian model is therefore an educational method which will encourage and support non-authoritarian individuals who are unwilling to bow to authority and who demand a social organization which provides them with maximum individual control and freedom.

An implicit assumption of the theories discussed in this volume is that changes in methods of education and child rearing can contribute to a radical transformation of society. This assumption raises questions about the value of these theories in our present society. Is it a waste of energy to direct one's concerns toward educational changes as a means of social change? Should one concentrate on other social and economic changes and let educational change follow in their wake? Will educational systems always be a mirror of the surrounding society?

One way of approaching these questions is to consider the social uses of public education in the United States in the nineteenth and twentieth centuries. In the first place, it is naive to assume that the educational systems *precisely* mirror the surrounding society. Society has never been homogeneous and without conflicting interests. There has never been a consensus about the goals and methods of public education. What has happened in fact is that the goals and methods of education have mirrored the goals and interests of those who have power in society.[2]

This situation has resulted in public education being used primarily as a conservative force for the solution of social problems. The use of public education as an instrument of social improvement has allowed people to act as if they were doing good without making any fundamental changes in society. In the nineteenth and twentieth centuries education has been viewed as a means of ending poverty, crime, and urban disorder by teaching the child in the schoolhouse proper social attitudes and work habits. This means the individual is told he or she is the problem and not that the *social system* needs to be changed. Everyone can rally around the flag of the schoolhouse without threatening the existing organization of society. Certainly, this was the situation in the 1960's when President Lyndon Johnson translated the demands of the civil rights movement into a theory of cultural deprivation, arguing that salvation from poverty and racism could be found in an improved educational system. When in the 1970's everyone awoke to the fact that the educational system had not eliminated racism or poverty, people began to argue that education had very little to offer in the way of social change.[3]

This conclusion is correct if one assumes that education's role is what Paulo Freire has called the banking system of education, which in fact tends to support social rigidity. Certainly the theories considered in this volume, however, connect changes in education to an ongoing program of social change. Part of their emphasis is that no social change is meaningful unless people participate in its formulation. And this applies, as well, to children.

THE WEDDING OF revolutionary thought to radical pedagogy had its roots in a profound pessimism, a feeling that revolutionary social and economic changes in the twentieth century had resulted in totalitarian states—the Soviet Union, for example, where revolutionary impulses were followed by a period of conservative dictatorship. Why the failure of this revolutionary endeavor? For people like Reich, Neill, and Freire the answer lies in its failure to provide radically new means of education and socialization by which all people could be brought into the revolutionary movement and become *acting members* of it rather than its objects.

From this perspective, a radical educational theory makes sense only if it is seen as part of a total revolutionary endeavor. One of the most serious problems facing the present and future development of libertarian forms of education is the dangerous separation of educational methods from a political and social ideology. Radical experiments in education tend to be trivialized as fast as they are developed. Paulo Freire's techniques are adopted by the Peace Corps and the free school methods of Summerhill are introduced into the classrooms of the public school without any relationship to their underlying radical ideology. What begins as a radical movement is quickly absorbed by the existing system; new techniques are used, but only to accomplish the old objectives of control and discipline. The Summerhillian approach, trivialized within the public school classroom, becomes a warm, loving, and free method of teaching the same subject matter and producing the same character structure.[4] One obvious example of this process is the movement for day-care centers. Once divorced from a movement to change the family and to free society from the authoritarian personality and state control, the day-care center becomes an instrument for dominating the population. Day-care centers are now being used as a means of controlling the poor by creating a new institutional family structure and by avoiding any major changes in the economic system by forcing the welfare mother to work. Day-care centers are provided not to relieve people from an authoritarian family structure, but to provide them with one that they are believed to lack.

The future of any radical endeavor in education depends upon maintaining the link between educational methods and a libertarian perspective. The social critique, the planning, and the methods must all be kept together.

Certainly, the greatness of John Dewey was his ability to link a psychological definition of humanity to a total social philosophy, and then to develop educational methods based on that concept of humanity and guided by that social philosophy. All methods and content in education affect character and action. Consequently, all educational techniques reflect some ideological position. For instance, Paulo Freire has certainly shown that the teaching of reading and writing might be the most political act in education. If education is pursued *without* a conscious radical perspective, it will do nothing but serve the existing social order.

It should also be clearly understood that there are two distinct ways of talking about education's potential to have a radical effect on society. On the one hand, educational systems such as Paulo Freire's can provide a method which liberates individuals so that they will act to bring about a radical change in society. On the other hand, an educational establishment itself may directly affect society, as in the case of a day-care center which weakens the family structure. Both approaches can be combined within one system. A.S. Neill's dream of a socialist state with Summerhill schools was directed both at weakening the family and at creating the self-regulated individual.

While the above arguments would seem to demonstrate that there *is* something called radical education which *can* have a meaningful role in radical social change, it does not answer the question of whether it is worthwhile to direct one's energies toward educational change rather than concentrating on other areas of social change. One reply, of course, could emphasize the essential role of educational change in any radical movement, as our theorists have stressed. But this reply avoids the problem of the existence of a tremendously powerful and complex educational establishment with its increasingly effective mechanisms for absorbing criticism and utilizing any educational method for its own purposes. This is not to suggest that there is any conspiratorial group manipulating the educational system. If this were true, the problem might be much simpler. In reality this educational establishment is a complex web of often competing groups. In the United States these groups range from professional teaching organizations and unions, through administrative organizations, schools of education, publishing companies, and testing organizations, to state legislatures, national policy groups, and the federal government.

Any attempt to make a radical pedagogy part of a radical political and social movement must come to terms with this educational establishment. The neglect of attempts to change this educational establishment would mean the neglect of an entire generation which is held in the custodial control of the school. Moreover, a very good case can be made for political and social movements to have to direct some energy toward educational change since the school is one of the major public institutions, second only to the Defense Department in terms of public expenditures. If we talk about change in our social institutions, we certainly cannot neglect one of the largest and most intrusive of them. In fact, it is the one public institution which has the most contact with all members of society.

The school, in short, must be approached first of all as a political and social institution. To give concrete meaning to theories of radical education—to that which *can be*—one must begin by coming to terms with that which *exists*. The one major shortcoming of radical educational theorists has been their failure to deal with the reality of existing educational systems and how their theories might be implemented. For instance, it is fine for A.S. Neill to establish a model like Summerhill, but Summerhill has little meaning unless it can be implemented throughout society. Neill was never very helpful about the strategies one might use to convert an entire educational system to that model. The failure of many free schools in the 1960's was a direct result of not making a concrete assessment of the political workings of public schooling and developing of strategies to confront and change that system. Many of these schools just languished outside the system, without money or power. What this means is that if radical pedagogy is to be made part of a radical movement, it can not act as if it were creating a new educational system in a vacuum. Strategies must be developed to confront the political realities of the existing educational establishment.

LET US CONSIDER some possible strategies for radicalizing American education. Any plan for meaningful educational change must affect the whole spectrum of educational power. There must not only be alternative educational models, but also a legal campaign to change educational laws, a fight for a different system of educational funding, an understanding of the need for children's rights, an emphasis on women's rights and changing the structure of the family, and a campaign to change the nature and direction of research in the schools of education of major universities.

One of the first steps that could be taken would be the elimination of compulsory education.[5] A campaign against compulsory education laws might be conducted, either through the courts or on the floor of state legislatures. No radical educational plan can really be developed if all children are required to attend a school approved by the state government. But at the same time compulsory education laws are attacked, it must be recognized that they were originally developed to solve certain social problems, namely child labor and juvenile delinquency. Compulsory education does protect children from economic exploitation and does serve the custodial function of occupying time. Thus, the end of compulsory education would have to be accompanied by a change in the economic structure which allowed for the financial independence of youth.

An economic change of this nature could have a direct effect upon the family. Because the increased duration of schooling has prolonged the child's dependency upon the family structure, heads of household must earn an income above their personal needs in order to support their dependents—children or other non-wage-earning members of the family. To alleviate this economic dependence on the family, the surplus income of the head of the household could be rechanneled to the children. This might involve a plan which would levy a tax on adults for the support of children. Accompanying this economic change could be changes in the legal rights of children. For instance, children might remain within the custody of the family until the age of twelve or thirteen. Up to that point the child's income from the state would be used as an educational voucher. The child and the family would make a decision about how the money should be used for educational purposes. This would break the monopoly of public schools and allow for the use of a wide variety of alternative schools. Then, at the age of thirteen or fourteen, youths would be recognized as being legally independent of the family and allowed to leave home if they so desired. Income would be guaranteed by the state until the age of twenty-one. Before the age of thirteen or fourteen children would be able to ask the courts to remove them from intolerable home situations.

Economic independence would allow for the changing of other laws affecting youth. Child labor laws could be eliminated because youths would no longer be vulnerable to exploitation on the labor market.[6] Youths could choose jobs because of interest and desire to learn. There could also be a campaign to insure adolescent sexual freedom. Not only could all restrictive laws be removed but birth-control devices and information might be provided. Economic independence and legal changes hopefully would overcome what Wilhelm Reich referred to as the "housing problems." Independent residences might be made available to youths. Society, in short, could recognize the legitimacy of adolescent sexual activity.

The economic independence of youth would represent a major step in the liberation of women. Traditionally, girls and young women have been under the control of the family for longer periods of time than their male counterparts. Even marriage at an early age only results in a shift from the control of one head of the household to another. A major source of female dependence on the family is the lack of easy access to occupations which provide economic independence. Combined with this economic problem is the traditional attitude that women must be protected by the home and denied the social independence of their male counterparts. Providing women with equal economic independence would hopefully allow them the same type of social freedom and opportunity for development.

The elimination of compulsory education and the shifting of educational funding from the level of the school to that of the individual could break the power of the educational bureaucracy. It should be recognized that in the United States, control of the school does not really reside in the local boards of education.[7] Such important educational issues as curriculum, content of textbooks, and requirements for teacher certification are decided within an interlocking educational bureaucracy which includes professional organizations, state officials, universities, and publishing companies—not to mention the new learning corporations like IBM and Educational Testing Services, which represent the most important and rapidly growing parts of this bureaucracy.

One way to weaken the power of this educational bureaucracy would be to avoid any supervision of educational spending, leaving decisions about how the money should be spent completely up to the individual. That would mean parental supervision until the child was twelve or thirteen; after that, the individual youth would have absolute control over the spending of the money. If a government body were established to supervise the spending, it would be likely to fall under the power of the same social and economic influences which have surrounded the school. Instead, we could develop a democratic system which placed control in the hands of the individual. The practice of freedom is the best exercise in learning how to use freedom. What little money might be lost or squandered at an individual level would be nothing compared to the amount of money wasted and squandered within the existing educational structure. The history of government control and regulation in the United States has been one of creating what has been called a "socialism for the rich." We could exercise a traditional American distrust for government organizations as sources of power for those in control, and instead place our faith in individual actions.

The demise of the existing educational structure could be accompanied by the recognition that the concept of the school is out of date in modern technological society. The schools in the nineteenth century was viewed not only as a source of social control but also as a center where all the materials of learning, books and teachers, could be concentrated. With mass media and urban living there is no reason why a person should not be able to learn the basic skills of reading, writing, and arithmetic just by growing and interacting within the community. Ivan Illich's *Deschooling Society* has certainly offered path-breaking suggestions in this direction.

One of the immediate questions that occur when it is suggested that the school be eliminated is: What happens to the poor? Is not the school their only hope? How will they learn growing up in a culture of poverty? Without the school will there not be even greater social class differences? In response, it should be clearly recognized that schooling has *not* eliminated poverty in the past nor will it in the future. To use the school to solve problems of poverty is to seek a conservative solution without directly changing the social structure which created poverty. It should also be recognized that schooling as a system of social selection has tended to *reinforce* the existing social class structure. But to get *rid* of the school is certainly not going to eliminate poverty. In other words, having schools or not having schools is not going to make that much difference because schools are not at the heart of the problem of poverty. But if the school were eliminated *and at the same time* children and youth were given economic independence, the problem of poverty would be confronted directly. Poor children would have enough money to explore and enjoy the advantages now reserved for the middle class.

The next question, of course, is whether the culture of poverty doesn't hinder and limit the type of choices made by the parents and youth. The answer, of course, is yes. But this "yes" must be qualified in two ways. First, the poor are better judges of how their educational money should be spent than the traditional leaders in the educational bureaucracy. Second, the legal and legislative campaign directed against compulsory education and educational funding could be accompanied by the radicalization of the schools of education in major universities. This would provide a center for dealing directly with the problems raised by a culture of poverty by utilizing community education programs based on methods like Paulo Freire's and by developing techniques of radical therapy.

The radicalization of faculties of education would involve completely changing their conception of their own function. The educators would have to raise a whole new set of questions—questions very different from those which have occupied traditional pedagogical theory. As Wilhelm Reich suggested in the 1920's, nothing of major consequence can be accomplished by treatment at an individual level. If repression exists on a society-wide level, the solution is not individual treatment but changing those social conditions and institutions which cause repression. Individual therapy is essentially conservative because it leaves untouched the source of the problem. The same difficulty exists with schools and the faculties of education which have served those schools. Treatment of social problems has tended to be at an individual and conservative level. There is an attempt to overcome the culture of poverty by treating the child within the confines of the school. The real solution lies in directly attacking the social conditions which keep a person from learning and growing in our society.

One of the major obstacles in radicalizing faculties of education will be their traditional relationship to the process of schooling. Education departments and schools of education have tended to see their function primarily as one of serving the needs of the public schools by supplying teachers and services. Very often a large number of university people studying education have come from the ranks of public schooling and consider the department of education as an extension of the public schools. Historically, that is the reason for the establishment of normal schools and colleges of education. The consequence of this process has been a severe limitation on the study and development of meaningful educational processes.

The results of this narrow focus are reflected in the various disciplines within education. Today all such disciplines are directed toward serving the schools. Teacher training is designed primarily to prepare a person to teach standard subjects within a public school classroom. The nature of education courses is governed by the requirements for state certification. Educational psychology as a discipline in education tends to focus on the psychology of classroom management. It sees itself as supplying the scientific tools for teaching within the classroom and managing a captive audience of students. Both the research and content of instruction are centered on learning within the context of the classroom. Educational sociology tends to follow the same path and concentrates on classroom and school social interaction and the handling of cultural differences within the school. The teaching of educational history, like United States history in the public schools, is largely a matter of selling certain ideas and beliefs. Educational philosophy has tended to get lost within the process of defining and clarifying the goals of public schooling.

Radical groups, students, and faculty could begin to place pressure on faculties of education to rechart the direction of American education.[8] This pressure could be applied internally, through the teaching and research of individual faculty members, and through the demand by students for a different type of educational program. Outside groups, such as alternative schools, could place pressure on the universities to supply the same types of services as are extended to the public schools. The demand could be made that universities *not* exclusively serve the needs of public schooling but begin to look at the educational process within the framework of a broad cultural perspective.

One of the first things that might be done would be to separate teacher training from the state certification requirements. This might initially involve proposing two separate courses of study in teacher training. One of these would lead to state certification and the other to the development and implementation of methods like Paulo Freire's. This second course of study would provide a base for the collection of material and training of workers for community action. Teachers trained in methods like Freire's could go into poverty areas and establish educational programs outside the public school system to develop social consciousness. The teacher training programs could also provide facilities for training minority group leaders, like Native Americans and blacks, in Freirian or other techniques.

Educational sociology and psychology could work together to accomplish what Wilhelm Reich called radical therapy. Both of these disciplines could begin to look at the problem of why certain people within our society cannot learn without relying upon the authoritarian structure of the school. If such dependency does not exist, we can safely abandon the school and rely on every individual to grow and learn in his or her own manner. But one suspects that at this stage, there are still many barriers to free and independent learning. This might be particularly true in cultures of poverty. The job for psychology and sociology would be to identify those barriers which create a state of dependency in the learning process. Is the problem, as Reich suggested, mainly centered around the existence of the nuclear family? Is the problem more directly related to the economic conditions of poverty? Is it a result of the structure and the conditions of our modern urban environment? These and a host of other questions immediately come to mind. Sociology and psychology could then go on to identify those social conditions which would allow people to live and grow in the world without the authoritarian control of the schools. They could develop a radical therapy which would result in major changes in our society. If children cannot learn, one must not stop with just helping them to overcome their immediate problem. One must identify those social conditions which hinder their learning and directly attack those conditions.

Educational sociology could also assume the extra burden of studying the nature of control and economic exploitation in education. At a local level studies need to be made of the relationship between local elites and control of education. Such studies, linking the ideology of the school with the ideology of a particular social class, would follow in the tradition of George Counts' early studies on the social composition of school boards. In addition, students might be mobilized to study the financial dealings of local school districts and watch for possible conflicts of interest. What needs to be done on a national level is a study of the national power elite in education. This would include a study of the educational leaders who move easily between foundations, publishing companies, universities, educational organizations, and the federal educational establishment. It would be interesting to study the ideology of this power elite and its effect upon education.

The history and philosophy of education could begin to study the relationship between ideology and educational practice which includes the whole socialization process. Any theory about the socialization process is based on a concept of human nature and directed toward a vision of what ought to be. Theories of the family, community, school, city planning, and other related parts of the socialization process would be defined in terms of these underlying ideologies. History and philosophy could make these ideological assumptions explicit, examining them both in their historical context and in their present manifestations. It should be the responsibility of these two disciplines to assure that educational methods do not become isolated from their political and social roots.

WHILE ALL THE ABOVE STRATEGIES are tentative, they do represent the kinds of practical things that must be considered if radical education is to have any meaning. There must be a clear development of how theory can be put into practice in the modern world. For years American educators have wondered why the educational philosophy of John Dewey has so little influence on the daily workings of the public school classroom. Part of the answer can be found in Dewey's own writings. While

Dewey certainly translated his philosophy into classroom methods, he never suggested ways the educational establishment could be changed so that his methods could be put into practice. Dewey's method became a topic of discussion but not a practical tool. In the same way, radical pedagogy could become just a topic for discussion unless it orients itself politically toward the realities of the existing educational structure.

One hundred years ago it would have been difficult to convince large numbers of people that changing educational institutions was a necessary part of political and economic change. Today this is equally true because social and economic forces have made schools one of the central controlling agencies in society. For this reason schools must become a part of any attempt at major social change. This does not necessarily mean an extension of schooling; it could as easily mean the limitation or elimination of schooling. What must be kept in mind is that mass schooling is a product of a particular set of historical forces which has made it into one of the major institutions for planned socialization.

What must also be kept in mind is the distinction between schooling and education. Schooling has been a planned method of socialization designed to produce obedient workers and citizens through a system of institutional controls. On the other hand, education can mean gaining knowledge and ability by which one can transform the world and maximize individual autonomy. Education can be a source of individual liberation. One of the internal contradictions within the present system of schooling relates to this distinction. Modern workers do need basic skills and some degree of understanding of the world and, consequently, must be given some education. It very often happens that this education raises the level of awareness enough to cause rebellion against the process of socialization or schooling. This has occurred in the last ten years in student protests and demands for protection of individual liberties and rights. Unfortunately this has occurred mainly in middle-class schools where there is still some semblance of education. Poor children have been primarily well schooled and not well educated.

Presently in the United States there is a movement to eliminate all vestiges of education in favor of something called "career education." The career education movement holds as a basic tenet of faith that all learning must be directed toward the needs of some future occupation. Learning is made subservient to a future social role and the socialization process of the school. Knowledge is not presented as a means of understanding and critically analyzing social and economic forces but as a means of subservience to the social structure. "Career education" could represent the logical outcome of the controlling power of schooling.[9]

What must be sought in the future is a system of education which raises the level of individual consciousness to an understanding of the social and historical forces that have created the existing society and determined an individual's place in that society. This must occur through a combination of theory and practice in which both change as all people work for a liberated society. There should not be a blueprint for future change but, rather, a constant dialogue about means and ends. Education should be at the heart of such a revolutionary endeavor.

FOOTNOTES

Chapter I

[1] Samuel Bowles, "Understanding Unequal Economic Opportunity,"*American Economic Review*, Vol. LXIII, No. 2, May 1973, pp. 346-356; Samuel Bowles and Herbert Gintis, "I.Q. in the U.S. Class Structure," *Social Policy*, Vol. 3, Nos. 4 and 5, Nov./Dec. 1972 and Jan./Feb. 1973; Samuel Bowles, "Schooling and Inequality from Generation to Generation," *Journal of Political Economy*, May/June 1972.

[2] A good biography and summary of Godwin's ideas is George Woodcock's *William Godwin* (London: The Porcupine Press, 1946).

[3] William Godwin, "An Account of the Seminary ... At Epsom in Surrey," in *Four Early Pamphlets* (Gainesville, Florida: Scholars' Facsimiles and Reprints, 1966), p. 150.

[4] William Godwin, *Enquiry Concerning Political Justice and its Influence on Morals and Happiness* (Toronto: The University of Toronto Press, 1946), Vol. II, p. 302.

[5] See Woodcock, *op. cit.*, pp. 63-73.

[6] Godwin, *Enquiry Concerning . . .* , Vol. II, pp. 302-303.

[7] *Ibid.*, Vol. II, p. 304.

[8] *Ibid.*

[9] See Johann Gottlieb Fichte, "The Nature of the New Education," in *Addresses to the German Nation*, trans. by R.F. Jones and G.H. Turnbull (Chicago: Open Court Publishing Co., 1922).

[10] See *Henry Barnard on Education* edited by John S. Brubacher (New York: McGraw-Hill, 1931), p. 74.

[11] This is taken from George Mosse's fine anthology of *Nazi Culture* (New York: Grosset & Dunlap, 1966).

[12] For further elaboration of radical reaction to schooling in the United States see Chapter VII of my book *Education and the Rise of the Corporate State* (Boston: Beacon Press, 1972).

[13] Francisco Ferrer, "L'Ecole Renovee," *Mother Earth* (Nov., 1909), Vol. IV, No. 9, p. 269.

[14] *Ibid.*, p. 268.

[15] *Ibid.*, p. 272.

[16] *Ibid.*

[17] Francisco Ferrer, *The Origin and Ideals of the Modern School*, trans. by Joseph McCabe (New York: G.P. Putnam's Sons, 1913), p. 48.

[18] Ferrer, "L'Ecole Renovée," p. 269.

[19] William Godwin, *The Enquirer* (London: C.G. & J. Robinson, 1797), pp. 66-97.

[20] Harry Kelly, "The Modern School in Retrospect," in *The Modern School of Stelton* (Stelton, New Jersey: The Modern School Association of North America, 1925), p. 115.

[21] For Ivan Illich's expansion of the concept of alienation see his paper *The Breakdown of Schools* (Cuernavaca, Mexico: CIDOC, Apr., 1971), pp. 11-19.

[22] See Wilhelm Reich, *The Mass Psychology of Fascism* (New York: Farrar, Straus and Giroux, 1970).

[23] See A.B. Hollinshead, *Elmtown's Youth* (New York: John Wiley & Sons, 1949).

Chapter II

[1] Francisco Ferrer, *The Origin and Ideals of the Modern School*, pp. 89-90.

[2] Jean Jacques Rousseau, *Emile* (New York: Dutton, 1911).

[3] For a biographical sketch of Stirner's life see George Wood-

cock's *Anarchism: A History of Libertarian Ideas and Movements* (Cleveland: The World Publishing Co., 1969), pp. 94-105.

[4] Max Stirner, *The Ego and His Own: The Case of the Individual Against Authority*, trans. by Steven T. Byington (New York: Libertarian Book Club, 1963), p. 342.

[5] Max Stirner, *The False Principle of Our Education*, trans. by Robert H. Beebe (Colorado Springs: Ralph Myles, 1967), p. 23.

[6] Stirner, *The Ego and His Own*, pp. 106-7.

[7] *Ibid.*, p. 242.

[8] *Ibid.*, p. 52, 342.

[9] *Ibid.*, pp. 330-335.

[10] *Ibid.*, pp. 200-209.

[11] *Ibid.*, pp. 173-185.

[12] Emma Goldman, "The Child and Its Enemies," *Mother Earth* (April, 1906), Vol. I, No. 2, pp. 12-13.

[13] Ferrer, *The Origin and Ideas of the Modern School*, pp. 76-87.

[14] *Ibid.*, p. 29.

[15] *Ibid.*, p. 76.

[16] *Ibid.*, pp. 86-89, 89-90.

[17] Goldman, "The Child and Its Enemies," p. 9.

[18] Leo Tolstoy, "Education and Culture," in *Tolstoy on Education*, trans. by Leo Wiener (Chicago: The University of Chicago Press, 1967).

[19] Stirner, *The False Principle of Our Education*, p. 23.

[20] *Ibid.*, pp. 1-25.

[21] Ivan Illich, "The Breakdown of Schools: a problem or a SYMPTOM?" (Cuernavaca, Mexico 71.04.21), pp. 11-19.

[22] Elizabeth Burns Ferm, "Activity and Passivity of the Educator," *Mother Earth* (March, 1907), Vol. II, No. 1, p. 26.

[23] Colin Ward, "Adventure Playground: A Parable of Anarchy," *Anarchy* 7 (1961), pp. 193-201.

[24] *Ibid.*

[25] George Dennison, "The First Street School," in *Radical School Reform*, edited by Ronald and Beatrice Gross (New York: Simon and Schuster, 1969), pp. 227-246.

[26] See Paul Goodman's *New Reformation: Notes of a Neolithic Conservative* (New York: Random House, 1970), and *Communitas* (New York: Random House, 1965).

[27] Paul Goodman, *Compulsory Mis-Education and The Community of Scholars* (New York: Vintage Books, 1966), p. 57.

149

[28] *Ibid.*, pp. 30-34.

[29] See Ivan Illich, *Celebration of Awareness: A Call for Institutional Revolution* (New York: Doubleday, 1971), and *De-Schooling Society* (New York: Harper & Row, 1971).

Chapter III

[1] Karl Marx and Friedrich Engels, *The German Ideology* (New York: International Publishers Inc., 1939), pp. 1-2.

[2] *Ibid.*, p. 14.

[3] Paulo Freire, *Pedagogy of the Oppressed*, trans. by Myra Berman Ramos (New York: Herder and Herder, 1970), p. 85.

[4] *Ibid.*, pp. 111-112.

[5] Karl Marx, *Economic and Philosophic Manuscripts*, trans. by T.B. Bottomore in Erich Fromm's *Marx's Concept of Man* (New York: Frederick Ungar Co., 1961), p. 101.

[6] *Ibid.*

[7] Rollo May, "The Emergence of Existential Psychology," in *Existential Psychology* edited by Rollo May (New York: Random House, 1960), p. 44.

[8] Freire, *Pedagogy of the Oppressed*, pp. 119-121.

[9] Marx, *The German Ideology*, p. 20.

[10] Karl Marx, *Capital*, trans. by Samuel Moore and Edward Aveling (London: Swan Sonnenschein and Co., Ltd., 1904), p. 423.

[11] John Dewey, *Democracy and Education* (New York: The Free Press, 1966), pp. 250-261.

[12] Freire, *Pedagogy of the Oppressed*, p. 59.

[13] Marx, *Economic and Philosophic Manuscripts*, p. 98.

[14] *Ibid.*, pp. 93-109.

[15] Marx, *The German Ideology*, p. 39.

[16] Paulo Freire, "The Adult Literacy Process as Cultural Action for Freedom," *Harvard Educational Review*, Vol. 40, 1970, No. 2, p. 216.

[17] Carl R. Rogers, *Client-Centered Therapy* (Boston: Houghton Mifflin Company, 1965), p. 488.

[18] *Ibid.*, p. 513.

[19] *Ibid.*, p. 522.

[20] Paulo Freire, *Pedagogy of the Oppressed*, pp. 119-186.

[21] See Murray Bookchin, *Post-Scarcity Anarchism* (Palo Alto: Ramparts, 1971).

[22] Paulo Freire, "Cultural Action and Conscientization," *Harvard Educational Review*, Vol. 40, 1970, No. 3, pp. 452-475.

Chapter IV

[1] A.S. Neill, "The Man Reich," in *Wilhelm Reich* by A.S. Neill, Paul and Jean Ritter, Myron Sharaf, Nic Wool (Nottingham: The Ritter Press, 1958), p. 21.
[2] See Sigmund Freud, *Civilization and Its Discontents* (London: Hogarth Press, 1949).
[3] Wilhelm Reich, *The Discovery of the Orgone: The Function of the Orgasm* (New York: Farrar, Straus and Giroux, 1970), p. 133.
[4] *Ibid.*, p. 53.
[5] Wilhelm Reich, *The Mass Psychology of Fascism*, p. 19.
[6] *Ibid.*, pp. 19-34.
[7] Reich, *The Discovery of Orgone . . .*, pp. 114-130.
[8] *Ibid.*, p. 124.
[9] *Ibid.* pp. 143-163.
[10] *Ibid.*, p. 156.
[11] *Ibid.*, p. 158.
[12] *Ibid.*, p. 153.
[13] Wilhelm Reich, *The Invasion of Compulsory Sex-Morality* (New York: Farrar, Straus and Giroux, 1971), p. 146.
[14] Wilhelm Reich, *The Sexual Revolution* (New York: Farrar, Straus and Giroux, 1962), p. 72.
[15] *Ibid.*, p. 77.
[16] *Ibid.*, p. 79.
[17] Reich, *The Mass Psychology of Fascism*, pp. 32, 55-59.
[18] *Ibid.*, pp. 68-74.
[19] *Ibid.*, p. 61.
[20] Reich, *The Sexual Revolution*, p. xiv.
[21] *Ibid.*, pp. 153-160.
[22] *Ibid.*, pp. 240-247.
[23] Reich, *The Invasion of Compulsory . . .*, pp. 9-10.
[24] Reich, *The Sexual Revolution*, pp. 243-246.
[25] *Ibid.*, p. 236.
[26] *Ibid.*, p. 237.
[27] Reich, *The Mass Psychology of Fascism*, p. 377.
[28] Wilhelm Reich, *The Murder of Christ* (New York: Farrar, Straus and Giroux, 1971).

[29] A.S. Neill, *The Problem Child* (New York: Robert M. McBride, 1927), pp. 18, 114.

[30] *Ibid.*, p. 52.

[31] A.S. Neill, *The Problem Family* (New York: Hermitage Press, 1949), p. 17.

[32] A.S. Neill, "The Man Reich," pp. 24-25.

[33] Neill, *The Problem Child*, p. 100.

[34] *Ibid.*, pp. 211, 231-232.

[35] A.S. Neill, "Authority and Freedom in the School," *The New Era*, 16:23 (January, 1935), pp. 22-25.

[36] A.S. Neill, *The Problem Teacher* (New York: The International Press, 1944), pp. 19-32.

[37] *Ibid.*, p. 27.

[38] A.S. Neill, *Hearts Not Heads in the School* (London: Herbert Jenkins Ltd., 1944), pp. 31-34.

[39] *Ibid.*, p. 21.

[40] Neill, *The Problem Family*, p. 177.

[41] *Ibid.*, p. 173.

[42] *Ibid.*, p. 151.

Chapter V

[1] Philippe Ariès, *Centuries of Childhood: A Social History of Family Life*, translated by Robert Baldick (New York: Vintage Books, 1962), p. 441.

[2] Frank Musgrove, *Youth and the Social Order* (London: Routledge and Kegan Paul, 1964).

[3] Clarence J. Karier, Paul Violas, and Joel Spring, *Roots of Crisis* (Chicago: Rand McNally, 1973).

[4] Melford E. Spiro, *Kibbutz* (New York: Schocken Books, 1970).

[5] *Ibid.*, p. 226.

[6] *Ibid.*, pp. 121-122.

[7] See David Rapaport, "The Study of Kibbutz Education and its Bearing on the Theory of Development," *American Journal of Orthopsychiatry*, XXVIII (1958), pp. 587-597 and Melford Spiro's *Children of the Kibbutz* (New York: Schocken Books, 1965).

[8] Bruno Bettelheim, *The Children of the Dream: Communal Child-Rearing and American Education* (New York: Avon Books, 1970), p. 145.

[9] *Ibid.*, p. 144.

[10] *Ibid.*, pp. 137-147.

[11] *Ibid.*, p. 281.

[12] *Ibid.*, pp. 188-193.

[13] Emma Goldman, *Anarchism and Other Essays* (New York: Dover Publications, Inc., 1969), pp. 214-225.

Chapter VI

[1] A study of the influence of this model on the development of education in the twentieth century can be found in Joel Spring's *Education and the Rise of the Corporate State* (Boston: Beacon Press, 1972) and in *Roots of Crisis* (Chicago: Rand McNally, 1973) by Clarence Karier, Paul Violas and Joel Spring. The effect of this model on the development of the high school is detailed in Edward Krug's *The Shaping of the American High School, Volume I* (New York: Harper & Row, 1964).

[2] For an introduction to how education has mirrored class interests see Michael B. Katz, *The Irony of Early School Reform* (Boston: Beacon Press, 1970) and Spring, *op. cit.*

[3] The most important government document which provided the basic arguments for the war on poverty and linked education with the solution of poverty and discrimination was "The Problem of Poverty in America," *The Annual Report of the Council of Economic Advisers* (Washington, D.C.: U.S. Printing Office, 1964).

[4] On the trivialization of radical school experiments see Jonathan Kozol's *Free Schools* (Boston: Houghton Mifflin, 1972).

[5] On the issue of compulsory schooling see *The Twelve Year Sentence* edited by William F. Rickenbacker (LaSalle, Illinois: Open Court, 1974).

[6] One position in this regard is clearly stated in John Holt's *Escape From Childhood* (New York: Dutton, 1974).

[7] See James Koerner's *Who Controls American Education?* (Boston: Beacon Press, 1968).

[8] One recent example of change in this direction is the 1975 yearbook of the Association for Supervision and Curriculum Development. This yearbook, *Schools in Search of Meaning* edited by James Macdonald and Esther Zaret (Washington, D.C.: Association for Supervision and Curriculum, 1975), contains a major radical critique of schooling by a group which has had very strong links with the public schools.

[9] The leading advocate of career education is former Commissioner of Education Sidney P. Marland. For an example of his thinking on the subject see his articles "The School's Role in Career Development," *Educational Leadership* 30, No. 3 (December 1972), pp. 203-205 and "The Endless Renaissance," *American Education* 8, No. 3 (April 1972), p. 9.

BIBLIOGRAPHY

Ariès, Philippe. *Centuries of Childhood: A Social History of Family Life*. New York: Vintage Books, 1962.

Bettelheim, Bruno. *The Children of the Dream: Communal Child-Rearing and American Education*. New York: The Macmillan Company, 1969.

Cohen, Joseph. *The Modern School of Stelton*. Stelton, New Jersey, 1925.

Ferrer, Francisco. "L'Ecole Renovée," *Mother Earth* (November, 1909).

The Origin and Ideals of the Modern School. New York: G.P. Putnam's Sons, 1913.

Freire, Paulo. "The Adult Literacy Process as Cultural Action for Freedom," *Harvard Educational Review*. Vol. 40, 1970, No. 2.

155

"Cultural Action and Conscientization," *Harvard Educational Review.* Vol. 40, 1970, No. 3.

Pedagogy of the Oppressed. New York: Herder and Herder, 1970.

Godwin, William. *The Enquirer.* London: C.G. and J. Robinson, 1797.

Enquiry Concerning Political Justice and Its Influence on Morals and Happiness. Toronto: The University of Toronto Press, 1946.

Four Early Pamphlets. Gainesville, Florida: Scholar's Facsimilis and Reprints, 1966.

Goldman, Emma. *Anarchism and Other Essays.* New York: Dover Publications, 1969.

Illich, Ivan. *Celebration of Awareness: A Call for Institutional Revolution.* New York: Doubleday, 1971.

De-Schooling Society. New York: Harper & Row, 1971.

Marx, Karl. *Capital.* Translated by Samuel Moore and Edward Aveling. London: Swann Sonnenschein & Co., Ltd., 1904.

Economic and Philosophic Manuscripts. Translated by T.B. Bottomore. In Erich Fromm's *Marx's Concept of Man.* New York: Frederick Ungar, 1961.

Marx, Karl and Friedrich Engels. *The German Ideology.* New York: International Publishers, Inc., 1939.

Neill, Alexander Sutherland. *Hearts Not Heads in the School.* London: Jenkins Limited, 1944.

The Problem Child. New York: Robert M. McBride & Company, 1927.

The Problem Teacher. New York: The International Press, 1944.

The Problem Family. New York: Hermitage Press, 1949.

Summerhill. New York: Hart Publ., 1960.

Willhelm Reich. Nottingham: The Ritter Press, 1958.

Reich, Wilhelm. *The Discovery of the Orgone: The Function of the Orgasm*. New York: Farrar, Straus and Giroux, 1970.

The Invasion of Compulsory Sex-Morality. New York: Farrar, Straus and Giroux, 1970.

The Mass Psychology of Fascism. New York: Farrar, Straus and Giroux, 1970.

The Sexual Revolution. New York: Farrar, Straus and Giroux, 1962.

Stirner, Max. *The Ego and His Own*. Translated by Steven T. Byington. New York: Libertarian Book Club, 1963.

The False Principle of Our Education. Translated by Robert Beebe. Colorado Springs: Ralph Myles, Publisher, 1967.

Tolstoy, Leo. *Tolstoy on Education*. Translated by Leo Wiener, Chicago: The University of Chicago Press, 1967.

Wollstonecraft, Mary. *A Vindication of the Rights of Woman*. London: Walter Scott.

ABOUT THE AUTHOR:
Joel Spring is an associate professor of education at Case Western Reserve University in Cleveland. He is author of *Education and the Rise of the Corporate State* and other books on education. He has written extensively for various educational and radical journals. Currently is he working on a study of national educational policy since World War II.

Free Life Editions would like to thank the following people who helped in various ways to make this book possible: Renna Draynel, Kathy Brown, Marcia Salo Rizzi, Walter Heitner and Faculty Press, our friends at Black Rose Books, and our own staff—Chuck Hamilton, Diane Radycki, Bertch, and Mark Powelson.

Ida Blechman